85-B 975

THE GODKIN LECTURES

ON THE ESSENTIALS OF FREE GOVERNMENT

AND THE DUTIES OF THE CITIZEN

were established at Harvard University in 1903 in memory of

EDWIN LAWRENCE GODKIN

1831–1902

They are given annually under the auspices

of the Harvard Graduate School of Public Administration

THE PUBLIC USE
of
PRIVATE INTEREST

CHARLES L. SCHULTZE

THE PUBLIC USE
of
PRIVATE INTEREST

THE BROOKINGS INSTITUTION
WASHINGTON, D.C.

Copyright © 1977 by
THE BROOKINGS INSTITUTION
1775 Massachusetts Avenue, N.W., Washington, D.C. 20036

Library of Congress Cataloging in Publication Data:

Schultze, Charles L
  The public use of private interest.
  Rev. and expanded version of the Godkin lectures
delivered at the John F. Kennedy School of Government,
Harvard University in Nov. and Dec. 1976.
  Includes bibliographical references and index.
  1. Government spending policy—United States.
2. Evaluation research (Social action programs)—United
States. 3. Supply and demand. I. Title. II. Series:
Godkin lectures, Harvard University; 1976.
HJ7539.S38   336.3'9'0973   77-8575
ISBN 0-8157-7762-0
ISBN 0-8157-7761-2 pbk.

1 2 3 4 5 6 7 8 9

THE BROOKINGS INSTITUTION is an independent organization devoted to nonpartisan research, education, and publication in economics, government, foreign policy, and the social sciences generally. Its principal purposes are to aid in the development of sound public policies and to promote public understanding of issues of national importance.

The Institution was founded on December 8, 1927, to merge the activities of the Institute for Government Research, founded in 1916, the Institute of Economics, founded in 1922, and the Robert Brookings Graduate School of Economics and Government, founded in 1924.

The Board of Trustees is responsible for the general administration of the Institution, while the immediate direction of the policies, program, and staff is vested in the President, assisted by an advisory committee of the officers and staff. The by-laws of the Institution state, "It is the function of the Trustees to make possible the conduct of scientific research and publication, under the most favorable conditions, and to safeguard the independence of the research staff in the pursuit of their studies and in the publication of the results of such studies. It is not a part of their function to determine, control, or influence the conduct of particular investigations or the conclusions reached."

The President bears final responsibility for the decision to publish a manuscript as a Brookings book or staff paper. In reaching his judgment on the competence, accuracy, and objectivity of each study, the President is advised by the director of the appropriate research program and weighs the views of a panel of expert outside readers who report to him in confidence on the quality of the work. Publication of a work signifies that it is deemed to be a competent treatment worthy of public consideration; such publication does not imply endorsement of conclusions or recommendations contained in the study.

The Institution maintains its position of neutrality on issues of public policy in order to safeguard the intellectual freedom of the staff. Hence interpretations or conclusions in Brookings publications should be understood to be solely those of the author or authors and should not be attributed to the Institution, to its trustees, officers, or other staff members, or to the organizations that support its research.

Foreword

THE AMERICAN PEOPLE are ambivalent about the role of government in society. On the one hand, they expect government to provide for the nation's security, ensure a decent income for the retired and the poor, give everyone equal access to a good education, improve the availability of health care and housing, build and maintain a national highway system, and promote economic growth and stability. On the other hand, there is a widespread view that government has become too big, too bureaucratic, and ineffective in dealing with the special problems of an advanced industrial society. Government often seems to fail when it tackles a critical issue, whether it is pollution abatement, energy conservation, urban renewal, occupational safety, or control of medical costs.

The failure does not seem to derive mainly from excessive government spending. It is true that outlays by state and local governments have risen sharply since the end of World War II, but the rise has been largely a response to the demands of a rapidly growing population; the expansion of state and local government spending is already tapering off as the rate of population growth has declined. At the federal level, government expenditures have remained at roughly a fifth of the gross national product for over two decades, except for periods of recession and their aftermath. The real difficulty has been that, as society has become more complex, government has been forced to intervene more and more in the activities and decisions of consumers and businessmen in order to achieve national objectives—and has done so almost exclusively with detailed laws and regulations. Such regulatory efforts have often been inefficient and sometimes have done more harm than good.

In this book Charles L. Schultze explains why public regulation of the private sector is inherently difficult, and how government intervention can be improved. His main thesis is that the regulatory laws and agencies have attempted directly to *force* people and businesses to do certain things rather than to *encourage* them through indirect methods to achieve the same objectives. He suggests, as an alternative, the use of market-like incentives—such as tax and transfer arrangements—that would convert public goals into private interests. Such incentives would remove some of the decisions from a central bureaucracy and rely on decentralized private markets to achieve the desired results.

This book is a revision of material presented in the Godkin Lectures at Harvard University in November and December 1976. The author, who was a Brookings senior fellow in economics when he prepared these lectures, was formerly director of the Bureau of the Budget and is currently chairman of the Council of Economic Advisers. He wishes to acknowledge the comments and criticisms of many friends and colleagues who read drafts of the manuscript: Henry J. Aaron, Edward R. Fried, Robert W. Hartman, Herbert Kaufman, Arthur M. Okun, Henry Owen, John L. Palmer, Joseph A. Pechman, and George L. Perry. Most of the research assistance was provided by Michael Klausner. Evelyn P. Fisher reviewed the final draft for accuracy and Mendelle T. Berenson edited the manuscript. The index was prepared by Brian Svikhart.

The views expressed in this book are those of the author and should not be ascribed to the trustees, officers, or other staff members of the Brookings Institution.

BRUCE K. MACLAURY
President

Washington, D.C.
July 1977

THE PUBLIC USE
of
PRIVATE INTEREST

I

ECONOMISTS DISTINGUISH three criteria for assessing economic performance: aggregate or macro-efficiency, measured principally in terms of total output, employment, and price stability; micro-efficiency, or the degree to which the economic system meets the manifold and constantly changing demands of individuals for public and private goods; and the distribution of income and wealth, which determines how these goods are apportioned among families and individuals. Most economic and social policies of government are interventions into the workings of the private market in an attempt to improve one or more of these three aspects of performance.

Eleven years ago Walter Heller devoted his Godkin lectures to government's role in dealing with the first goal—prosperity and price stability. Two years ago Arthur Okun analyzed the tension between the goal of an equitable income distribution and the goals of macro- and micro-efficiency. In this book I want to explore the growing problem of social intervention at the micro-level: when and how should government intervene in private markets for the purpose of improving economic efficiency?

The term "efficiency" carries far more freight in the economist's vocabulary than in normal parlance. It does not simply mean producing and distributing goods cheaply. Rather it is a measure of how well society meets—in quality and quantity—the material wants of its members. An economic system that produced large quantities of unwanted low-cost goods would not be efficient.

Economic efficiency as applied to government has several dimensions. Some goods—like police protection and basic

1

health research—will not be produced in appropriate amounts, if at all, by a private market system; so an efficient economy requires government production or purchases of such public goods. Buyers should have sufficient knowledge to match their preferences with product characteristics; otherwise, constraints may have to be placed on product quality and safety. The legal system specifies laws of liability and contract that affect how much effort individuals and firms will take to avoid accidents or produce reliable products. Apart from transfer payments made to redistribute income, most of the domestic spending of government and most of its regulation is concerned with economic efficiency as defined in these ways.[1]

Casual observation, the findings of opinion surveys, and the political rhetoric of the 1976 election campaign suggest that the public has become disenchanted with the ability of government, especially the federal government, to function effectively. During the 1960s the belief took hold that some kind of federal budgetary program or federal regulatory agency could be designed to deal with almost any social or economic problem—deteriorating central cities, juvenile delinquency, low reading scores of poorer children, rat infestation, unsafe lawnmowers, and inefficient police departments. Scores of programs were enacted to deal with such problems. This belief of a few years ago now seems to have been replaced by its polar opposite: most federal programs do not work well and consist principally of "throwing money at problems." In a similar vein, the rash of new regulatory mechanisms established in recent years—for pollution control, energy conservation, industrial health and safety, consumer-product quality and safety, and the like—have generated a backlash of resentment against excessive red tape and bureaucratic control.

1. Such spending or regulation also affects income distribution. And often domestic spending or regulation, nominally undertaken for efficiency's sake, is actually motivated by a desire to affect the distribution of income. The impossibility of separating the efficiency from the income-distribution consequences of social intervention constitutes a major part of the problems with which this book will deal.

As always, however, contradictory themes run through public debate and public perceptions about government's capability to intervene effectively. During the controversy on the energy crisis, there was wide public support for tough federal controls on energy prices and oil companies. It was a Republican administration that proposed a $100 billion program of loans, guarantees, and investments for the energy industry. Polls reveal that a large majority of the public believe that the federal government has a responsibility for ensuring a decent income for the poor, seeing that jobs are available for those wanting work, and controlling inflation.[2] There seems to be substantial support for some form of national health insurance which, it can be predicted, will expand federal regulation of the health care industry. At the local level, decisions about land use, mineral exploration, and plant location are increasingly subjected to governmental scrutiny and influence with apparent popular approval.

This canvas of clashing colors is probably an accurate portrayal of underlying reality. On the one hand, the growing industrialization, urbanization, and interdependence of society generate an array of problems that cannot be handled by the purely voluntary buy-and-sell mechanism of private markets. Private markets cannot make it possible for individuals to buy clean rivers, uncongested city streets, safe neighborhoods, protection from exotic chemicals, or freedom from discriminatory practices. Growing affluence raises the expectations of the average citizen, and reduces his tolerance for the unpleasant side effects of economic growth. When the procurement of food, shelter, and clothing is still a struggle, environmental quality, neighborhood amenities, and safe workplaces rank well down the list of urgent demands. But they move toward the top when the struggle eases. Moreover, the burgeoning technical capability of modern societies also lifts expectations and lowers tolerance for imperfections. If a man can be put

2. The Harris Survey, March 1976 (data provided by Louis Harris & Associates).

on the moon, why can't cheap, clean solar power be provided? If the secret of life in DNA can be unraveled, why can't drugs without harmful side effects be developed? Finally, perhaps nourished by growing affluence, a new sense of social justice for racial minorities and women occasions all sorts of collective intervention into the detailed workings of the marketplace.

There is a growing body of objective evidence that government is not performing its new tasks effectively. The counterproductivity of governmental regulation of transportation is well documented.[3] Efforts to improve the environment, while far from a failure, are unnecessarily expensive and increasingly bogged down in Rube Goldberg regulations, legal snarls, and games between regulators and industry as enforcement deadlines draw near.[4] While Medicare and Medicaid have improved access to health care for the poor and the aged, government attempts to deal with rapidly escalating health costs have produced only burgeoning volumes of regulations and no results. Professional evaluations of manpower training, work experience, and related federal job programs usually find that their payoffs are low.[5] Although the compilation of absurdities perpetrated in the name of industrial safety often emanates from suspect sources—the industries being regulated—even the sympathetic observer finds it hard to recognize many of the regulations as anything *but* absurdities. The current debate over long-term energy policy shows how very difficult it is for government to deal with complicated price and resource-allocation problems.

3. George W. Douglas and James C. Miller III, *Economic Regulation of Domestic Air Transport: Theory and Policy* (Brookings Institution, 1974); George C. Eads, *The Local Service Airline Experiment* (Brookings Institution, 1972).

4. For a discussion of the problems that led to postponement of auto emission standards, see Allen V. Kneese and Charles L. Schultze, *Pollution, Prices, and Public Policy* (Brookings Institution, 1975), pp. 64–66.

5. *Studies in Public Welfare,* paper 3: *The Effectiveness of Manpower Training Programs: A Review of Research on the Impact on the Poor,* Prepared for the Subcommittee on Fiscal Policy of the Joint Economic Committee, 92:2 (Government Printing Office, 1972).

Conservatives believe that the whole set of recent social interventions is a big mistake. The cures have been worse than the disease: both the efficacy of the former and the seriousness of the latter have been overstated. Just as a circle cannot be squared or an angle trisected, so government intervention can never be made efficient. Ideally, much of the recent interventionist machinery should be dismantled; at a minimum no more should be added.[6]

An alternative view holds that there is nothing inherently wrong in the recent trend of interventionism. Most problems could be straightened out by reforming election laws, reducing the influence of special interests, electing honest and intelligent politicians, appointing capable administrators, undertaking thorough and comprehensive policy analyses, and devoting more money to underfunded programs.

While these are undoubtedly caricatures of two views, they do represent the kernel of the debate between "conservatives" and "liberals" about social intervention in the private sector. There is no denying the virtues of clean elections, competent officials, and professional analysis of social programs. And a healthy skepticism about the efficacy of collective cures for all social ills is surely warranted. But neither of these approaches is very helpful, or indeed relevant, in dealing with reality.

[The basic theme of this book is that there is a growing need for collective influence over individual and business behavior that was once the domain of purely private decisions. But as a society we are going about the job in a systematically bad way that will not be mended simply by electing and appointing more competent public officials or doing better analysis of public programs. First, a satisfactory method of sorting out the frivolous from the important occasions for intervention

6. Some conservative thought has gone beyond this. James M. Buchanan and others among the school of "public choice" economists argue that without radical new sets of constitutional restraints, majoritarian and logrolling rules of decisionmaking in the public sector will inevitably generate more of the same welfare-destroying intervention. See Buchanan's *The Limits of Liberty: Between Anarchy and Leviathan* (University of Chicago Press, 1975), and pp. 66–67 below.

has not been developed, and thus much social effort is spent to achieve such goals as having all fire extinguishers in industrial workplaces painted red. Second, we have a propensity to intervene in resource-allocation decisions in order to achieve equity and income-distribution goals that might better be handled by some form of tax or monetary-transfer arrangements. Finally, and perhaps most important, we usually tend to see only one way of intervening—namely, removing a set of decisions from the decentralized and incentive-oriented private market and transferring them to the command-and-control techniques of government bureaucracy. With some exceptions, modifying the incentives of the private market is not considered a relevant alternative. For a society that traditionally has boasted about the economic and social advantages of Adam Smith's invisible hand, ours has been strangely loath to employ the same techniques for collective intervention. Instead of creating incentives so that public goals become private interests, private interests are left unchanged and obedience to the public goals is commanded.

Collective intervention is not the same thing as collective coercion. While some element of coercion is implicit in any social intervention, the use of market-like incentives to achieve public purposes minimizes that element. And simultaneously, in dealing with complicated social interactions, incentives are more likely than centralized regulations to achieve effective and efficient results.

It is no small thing in a far-flung nation of over 200 million people to subject some sphere of private life to collective coercion. There are inevitable costs both in economic efficiency and in the scope of individual choice. Precisely because the legitimate occasions for social intervention will continue to multiply as society becomes more complex, congested, and technologically sophisticated, the collective-coercion component of intervention should be treated as a scarce resource. Since some coercion is implicit in all social intervention, intervention should be reserved for times when it promises large benefits. And when we do intervene we ought to maximize the use of techniques that modify the structure of private incentives rather than those that rely on the command-and-control approach of centralized bureaucracies.

In 1929, one hundred and forty years after the birth of the Republic, some 9 percent of the gross national income was spent by federal, state, and local governments for purposes other than national defense and foreign affairs. Between 1929 and 1960, however, the proportion of gross national income spent for domestic programs rose to 17½ percent. Today, only sixteen years later, that figure is 28 percent. Interest on the debt and cash transfers for direct income support to individuals now make up about one-third of those expenditures. The remainder represents some form of government delivery of goods and services or provision of subsidies. The fraction of the gross national income taken for these purposes by the federal government itself was about 1 percent of national income in 1929, grew to 2.8 percent by 1960, and rose to 6.5 percent by 1976.[7]

The growth of federal regulatory activities has been even more striking. There is no good way to quantify regulatory growth, but a few figures will illustrate its speed. Even as late as the middle 1950s the federal government had a major regulatory responsibility in only four areas: antitrust, financial institutions, transportation, and communications.[8] In 1976, eighty-three federal agencies were engaged in regulating some aspect of private activity.[9] Thirty-four of those had been created since 1960 and all but eighteen since 1930. By one count about 100,000 federal employees are engaged in regulatory ac-

7. These figures include federal grants-in-aid to state and local governments.

8. There were other regulatory activities—for example, meat inspection and food and drug regulation—but at the time their impact on the economy was small.

9. Any such count is necessarily somewhat arbitrary. The one used here is taken from the list submitted by the White House to the Congress as supporting material for the Agenda for Government Reform Act, proposed to the Congress by President Ford on May 13, 1976.

tivity.[10] The number of laws establishing or expanding regulatory activities has grown faster than the number of agencies. In the highly publicized case of the discharge of the toxic chemical Kepone into the public sewage system of Hopewell, Virginia, for example, four different federal regulatory laws were potentially applicable to the situation, all written in 1970 or later: the Clean Air Amendments of 1970; the Federal Water Pollution Control Act Amendments of 1972; the Federal Environmental Pesticide Control Act of 1972; and the Occupational Safety and Health Act of 1970. The compilation of regulations governing the Medicare program runs to 342 pages. Under the 1972 Federal Water Pollution Control Act Amendments, the Environmental Protection Agency is charged with establishing effluent limitations, and issuing effluent permits, for some 62,000 point sources of water pollution.

[Even more relevant to the theme of this book than the growing extent of governmental intervention is its changing nature, especially in the case of the federal government.] Until recently, federal intervention not only was limited in extent, but was carried out in a relatively uncomplicated way. The decision in the 1930s to launch a compulsory social security program represented a major political watershed. To reach it, important value conflicts had to be compromised or overridden. But once the decision was made, carrying it out efficiently—getting checks in the mail for the right amounts to the right people—was essentially simple. Undertaking to build what has turned out to be the $100 billion interstate highway system was no small decision. And it has had far-reaching effects on almost every aspect of American economic and social life. Yet again, in the earlier stages of the program, when most of the highways were constructed in rural areas, its execution was relatively straightforward. It is only recently that the pro-

10. "Estimated Employment in Government Regulatory Agencies, June 30, 1975," tabulation included in supporting material for the Agenda for Government Reform Act.

gram began to be beset by major complexities as it came to impinge on metropolitan areas, and on other government programs.

More generally, until perhaps fifteen or twenty years ago most federal activities in the domestic sphere were confined to a few broad areas: providing cash income under social security programs for which eligibility was fairly easily determined; investing in the infrastructure in a few sectors of the economy, principally highways, water resources, and high-rise public housing; regulating selected industries allegedly to control monopoly or prevent certain abuses; and operating various housekeeping activities such as the Post Office, the national parks, the merchant seamen's hospitals, and the air navigation system. But in the short space of twenty years the very nature of federal activity has changed radically. Addressed to much more intricate and difficult objectives, the newer programs are different; and the older ones have taken on more ambitious goals.

In the field of energy and the environment the generally accepted objectives of national policy imply a staggeringly complex and interlocking set of actions, directly affecting the production and consumption decisions of every citizen and every business firm. Consider for a moment the chain of collective decisions and their effects just in the case of electric utilities. Petroleum imports can be conserved by switching from oil-fired to coal-fired generation. But barring other measures, burning high-sulfur Eastern coal substantially increases pollution. Sulfur can be "scrubbed" from coal smoke in the stack, but at a heavy cost, with devices that turn out huge volumes of sulfur wastes that must be disposed of and about whose reliability there is some question. Intermittent control techniques (installing high smokestacks and switching off burners when meteorological conditions are adverse) can, at lower cost, reduce local concentrations of sulfur oxides in the air, but cannot cope with the growing problem of sulfates and widespread acid rainfall. Use of low-sulfur Western coal would avoid many of these problems, but this coal is obtained by strip mining. Strip-mine reclamation is possible, but substantially hindered in large areas of the West by lack of rainfall. Moreover, in some coal-rich areas the coal beds form the underground aquifer and their removal could wreck adjacent farming or ranching economies. Large coal-burning plants might be located in remote areas far from highly populated urban centers in order to minimize the human effects of pollution. But such areas are among the few left that are unspoiled by pollution, and both environmentalists and the residents (relatively few in number compared with those in metropolitan localities but large among the voting population in the particular states) strongly object to this policy. Fears, realistic or imaginary, about safety and about accumulation of radioactive waste have increasingly hampered the nuclear option. Court actions have delayed site selections, and increasingly stringent safety requirements and certification procedures have slowed construction and increased costs.

Complex as is this bare-boned outline, it deals with the case of public utilities, which has a much simpler environmental problem than that in many other fields. There are only about 1,000 electric utility plants, whose major environmental problems, nuclear aside, are confined to sulfur, particulates, and in some cases thermal pollution. But there are 62,000 point sources of water pollution, discharging a much larger variety of known, and probably some as yet unknown, pollutants. There are 100 million pollution-emitting vehicles on the road, whose contribution to the environmental problem depends not only on the particular pollution controls built into the vehicle but on the density of traffic, the time of day, local atmospheric conditions, the tuning of older engines, and the speed of travel.

The federal government has recently entered in a big way the field of regulating health and safety in workplaces throughout the country. The complexities of controlling industrial accidents, and over the longer run the even greater problem of identifying and dealing with industrial health problems in a chemically inventive society, are as great as those of energy and the environment.

On a quite different plane, over the last twenty years the federal government has become deeply involved for the first time in what might loosely be called social investments and social services. It not only provides heavy financial support for health care through Medicare and Medicaid, but actively seeks to influence the structure of the private health care system—through those programs, through manipulating its support of medical schools, and through various grant-in-aid programs. And the nation appears to be edging toward some sort of comprehensive national system of health insurance, more for the purpose of gaining social control over the health care system than of providing better financial insurance. Twenty years ago there were virtually no federal manpower programs; now we spend $9 billion a year on such programs and at least attempt to influence the very structure of national labor markets.

Even the goals of older programs have become more ambitious and correspondingly more complex. The purpose of federal highway grants in the late 1950s and early 1960s was simple: to help finance a highway network that would transport people and goods safely and conveniently from one place to another. Now the federal government, by making comprehensive transportation and urban development plans a condition of highway and mass-transit grants, at least attempts to deal with the broader problems of transportation and even beyond that to influence urban structure and growth. Early efforts to introduce federal aid to education sprang from a simple desire to provide more money. Now we ask why the subsequently enacted federal education programs are not more successful in improving test scores and other measures of achievement.

Until very recently most of the tasks undertaken by federal intervention were simple enough to be organized along typical bureaucratic lines. Once a program was enacted the details of its operations could be formulated and appropriate commands issued by highly centralized command centers. Dams could be built, social security records and check payments organized, and national parks run more or less by paying government employees to carry out preassigned tasks. There were, of course, important problems of public administration: civil service rules on hiring, firing, and promotion; organizational structures to avoid too much or too little control; appropriate accounting and auditing, and so forth. But the question was a narrow one: how to administer the relatively straightforward operations of the government itself.[11]

The single most important characteristic of the newer forms of social intervention is that their success depends on affecting the skills, attitudes, consumption habits, or production patterns of hundreds of millions of individuals, millions of business firms, and thousands of local units of government. The tasks are difficult, not so much because they deal with technologically complicated matters as because they aim ultimately at modifying the behavior of private producers and consumers. The boundaries of the "public administration" problem have leapt far beyond the question of how to effectively organize and run a public institution and now encompass the far more vexing question of how to change some aspect of the behavior of a whole society.

Societies that organize their entire productive sector along command-and-control lines do not, in the most fundamental sense, have a "problem" of how best to intervene to accomplish new tasks; there is no separate institutional mechanism in which to intervene. They simply add new commands and

11. The principal exception to this description was federal regulation of transportation. Here the ultimate actors were not government employees but private railroads, airlines, trucking firms, and barge lines. And it is precisely here that the most abysmal failure of government intervention has occurred. The federal government's powers, originally granted to prevent monopolistic practices, not only have failed in that purpose but in fact have been used to protect—indeed, to create—such practices. To a much lesser degree the same thing can be said of at least some aspects of federal regulation of financial institutions.

controls to the existing array. Whatever was good or bad, efficient or inefficient, about this form of social organization
before will not be changed significantly by the new task. But
in a society that relies on private enterprise and market incentives to carry out most productive activity, the problem of
intervention is a real one. Once the decision to intervene has
been taken, there remains a critical choice to be made: should
intervention be carried out by grafting a specific command-
and-control module—a regulatory apparatus—onto the system
of incentive-oriented private enterprise, or by modifying the
informational flow, institutional structure, or incentive pattern of that private system? Neither approach is appropriate to
every situation. But our political system almost always chooses
the command-and-control response and seldom tries the other
alternatives, regardless of whether that mode of response fits
the problem.[12] Analyzing the reasons for that bias, estimating
its costs and consequences, and suggesting areas in which the
alternative that embodies incentives, information, and institution building would be superior, form the principal tasks of
these lectures.

The very use of the term "social intervention" assumes a
good deal. It implies the "rebuttable presumption" that the
desirable mode of carrying out economic and social activities is
through a network of private and voluntary arrangements—
called, for short, "the private market." A theory of social intervention is thus concerned with defining the conditions under
which that presumption is indeed rebuttable. We think of the
public sector as intervening in the private sector, and not vice
versa.[13]

12. The major exception to the almost invariable choice of command
and control lies in our propensity to jigger the income tax code to generate
various special incentives. Ironically, the incentives provided are usually
the worst route to the goal. Just any old incentive won't do.
13. The nature of our rebuttable-presumption approach is far from
self-evident, however. In most societies throughout history (and in many
today), the presumption ran the other way. With only a little facetious-
ness, Lenin's New Economic Policy of the early 1920s, and the current
attempts to introduce profit-like calculations into Eastern European
economies, might be labeled "private intervention into the collective sys-

In the United States, reform movements and interventionist policies have seldom questioned the basic rebuttable presumption. The strong populist streak that runs through U.S. reformist history, and is still reflected in the rhetoric of politics, always meant that small businessmen and family farmers were high on the hero list. Populism sought to help its heroes with cheap money and by breaking up or regulating monopolies, not by nationalizing them. Even the Tennessee Valley Authority was sold as a "yardstick" for privately owned utilities, not as the first step toward public ownership.[14]

The rebuttable-presumption approach is also an implicit philosophical underpinning of modern welfare economics. The theory of social intervention for purposes of micro-efficiency (as distinct from income redistribution) is built upon three pillars: an analysis of the formal characteristics of an efficient economic system (Pareto optimality); a specification of the conditions under which a decentralized market system with private ownership of property will duplicate those characteristics (the duality conditions); and an identification of the situations in which existing private markets do not or cannot meet those conditions (market failure).[15]

Paradoxically, however, the rebuttable-presumption hypothesis has provided little guidance for the social intervention that has actually occurred, except to rule out nationalization of industry. There is little connection between the hypothesis as worked out by modern welfare theory and its application to social legislation. Once a political battle to intervene has been won in some broad area—environmental control, reduction of industrial accidents, or standards for nursing homes and day care centers—the extent and scope of the resulting social con-

---

tem." Until recently the social democratic parties of Western Europe maintained socialism as the ultimate goal of economic reform.

14. The regional structure and ownership of the Federal Reserve System reflects the positive distrust of large agglomerations, even if nationalized.

15. Actually, the term "market failure" is reserved for a certain subclass of the situations in which private markets do not or cannot meet the duality condition. But semantics are unimportant at the moment.

trols are seldom grounded in an analysis of where and to what extent the private market has failed to meet acceptable standards. Similarly, there is seldom any attempt to design techniques of intervention that preserve some of the virtues of the free market, which presumably justify the underlying rebuttable presumption. The usual approach to social control does not involve devising incentives, creating market analogs, or promoting competitive institutions. Apart from income-maintenance programs, the techniques of intervention are confined to centralized regulatory bodies, governmental delivery of free services, and categorical grants to subordinate units of government.

Elements of the paradox even seep into the way economic theory is constructed. The theoretical apparatus for identifying situations in which market failure occurs is quite elaborate. And the formal models of cost-benefit analysis, for the purpose of determining whether intervention is worthwhile, have been constructed with rigor. But the effort that has gone into theoretical and applied analysis of how to create or utilize decentralized mechanisms for social intervention has been, with a few exceptions, rather limited.

To some extent both political action and economic theory treat the instruments of social intervention as black boxes. First, one identifies a market failure—environmental pollution or industrial accidents or a mismatch between jobs and people in the labor market. Then, if the political system can generate a consensus that some form of social intervention is called for, the job is turned over to a black box, within which presumably omniscient and disinterested bureaucrats determine what is to be done and issue the necessary directives.

It is ironic indeed that a society whose citizens absorb the praises of the market's libertarian and economic virtues with their mothers' milk, and an economics profession that cut its teeth on demonstrating how a decentralized incentive system can produce socially desirable outcomes, should give such short shrift to those same concepts when it comes to forging tools for collective action.

II

WE ACKNOWLEDGE the power of economic incentives to foster steadily improving efficiency, and we employ it to bring us whitewall tires, cosmetics, and television sets. But for something really important like education, we eschew incentives. We would laugh if someone suggested that the best way to reduce labor input per unit of production was to set up a government agency to specify labor input in detail for each industry. But that is precisely how we go about trying to reduce environmental damage and industrial accidents.

Quite apart from the maximizing characteristics elaborated in formal economic theory, the buyer-seller relationships of the marketplace have substantial advantages as a form of social organization.

In the first place, relationships in the market are a form of unanimous-consent arrangement. When dealing with each other in a buy-sell transaction, individuals can act voluntarily on the basis of mutual advantage. Organizing large-scale social activity through the alternative open to a free society—democratic majoritarian politics—necessarily implies some minority who disapprove of each particular decision.[1] Everything else

1. One might argue in the contractarian tradition that there can exist at the "constitutional" level a virtually unanimous agreement to adopt a specific set of rules and constraints for political decisionmaking. In agreeing to the long-term arrangement each person expects the cumulative total of all decisions to benefit him. To provide for decision rules in cases in which buy-sell arrangements cannot work well, such a unanimous-consent interpretation of political decisionmaking may have merit. But that does not vitiate the point that, everything else being equal, unanimous consent in each particular decision is superior to unanimous consent only at the "constitutional" level. Moreover, as Arrow has shown, it is impossible to devise a set of political decision rules that are both non-dictatorially imposed and logically consistent. Kenneth J. Arrow, *Social Choice and Individual Values* (2d ed., Wiley, 1963).

being equal, unanimous-consent arrangements are much more attractive politically than any alternative. Obviously, everything else is not always equal. If the income distribution is grossly unfair, the concept of voluntary decisions and unanimous consent is a charade; necessity is no less coercive for being economic instead of political. Quite apart from income distribution, some kinds of decisions cannot be efficiently carried out under individual buy-sell arrangements—whence the body of economic analysis dealing with market failure. And finally, market transactions cannot take place at all without a prior stipulation by political means of property rights and definitions, which in turn strongly influences the efficiency and the distribution of gains from trade. But my point is not that the unfettered market is always superior, but rather that its buy-sell arrangements have a great social advantage. In designing techniques for collective intervention, the gains from preserving some or all of those arrangements should be given significant weight. Occasions to do so come up all the time: If government is to assist higher education, should it aid individual students who can then "buy" education where they choose or should it directly subsidize colleges and universities? Should federal manpower-training subsidies take the form, as they do now, of grants to institutions or of vouchers to individuals, à la the GI Bill of Rights? Should the federal government detail safety regulations for each industrial workplace or should it put a stiff price on industrial accidents (for example, via an injury-rate tax) and let individual firms decide how to respond in order to reduce their tax bills? To urge that the principle of voluntary decisions should be given weight is not to make it the sole criterion. But precisely because the legitimate occasions for social intervention will increase as time goes on, preserving and expanding the role of choice take on added importance.

Market-like arrangements not only minimize the need for coercion as a means of organizing society; they also reduce the need for compassion, patriotism, brotherly love, and cultural solidarity as motivating forces behind social improvement. Societies seeking to achieve a high standard of living have three major options in organizing individual citizens toward that end: coercion (by democratic majority rule or authoritarian dictate), self-interest incentives, and what we might loosely call the "emotional" forces listed above. Every society relies on some combination of the three, but in the matter of emphasis there are vast differences. Maoist China is unique in placing its chips heavily on cultural solidarity and an encompassing egalitarianism. It is far too early to tell whether this approach will succeed, and what its costs will be. Far less than China, but far more than the West, Japan relies on cultural solidarity as a principle of social organization. In any event, cultural solidarity as a central organizing theme is hardly relevant for Western nations, especially the United States with its heterogeneous ethnic population. And, however vital they may be to a civilized society, compassion, brotherly love, and patriotism are in too short supply to serve as substitutes. Harnessing the "base" motive of material self-interest to promote the common good is perhaps *the* most important social invention mankind has yet achieved. Turning silk into a silk purse is no great trick, but turning a sow's ear into a silk purse does indeed partake of the miraculous. In the abstract we accept that view, but sometimes in discussing the specifics of social intervention we are loath to apply it. If I want industry to cut down on pollution, indignant tirades about social responsibility can't hold a candle to schemes that reduce the profits of firms who pollute. If I want drivers to economize on gasoline usage, advertising appeals to patriotism, warnings about the energy crisis, and "don't be fuelish" slogans are no match for higher prices at the gas pumps. In most cases the prerequisite for social gains is the identification, not of villains and heroes but of the defects in the incentive system that drive ordinary decent citizens into doing things contrary to the common good. There is indeed a role for "preaching" as a means of creating a political and cultural climate in which consensus can be reached on social intervention. Cleaning up the environment will be achieved only as environmental quality takes a higher place in the value system of most citizens. But when it comes to the specifics of getting the job done, preaching, indignation, and identification of villains get in the way of results.

2.   A second advantage of the market as an organizing principle for social activity is that it reduces the need for hard-to-get information. Because we are paying out large sums to improve teacher-pupil ratios, enrich curricula, and build facilities, we want to know the relation between these factors on the one hand and educational results on the other—that is, to determine a production function for education. Consequently, we think it a major problem that educational research has failed to come up with any evidence that convincingly tells us what will make Johnny read better. There are a number of reasons for this failure, but chief among them is our inability to define and measure either the inputs or results of education satisfactorily. Why don't we also worry about our inability to find a production function for the output of the recreation industry? One reason is that its inputs and outputs are as hard to measure as those in education. What, for example, constitutes a satisfactory "recreational experience"? But the difficulty in answering is beside the point; in fact, we do not even ask the question, except perhaps in making decisions about public parks. The reason lies in the fact that most recreation is provided by the private market. Because individuals can choose freely, the prices that millions of them are willing to pay reflect the values they put upon various forms of recreation. Moreover, as far as the efficient provision of recreation for society as a whole is concerned, even individual sellers of recreational opportunities do not, in any formal sense, need to know their own production functions. Those who provide what the public is willing to pay for at costs that permit a reasonable profit survive; the others do not. To the extent that individual sellers do not know the precise shapes of demand and cost curves, the Darwinian selection process may waste some resources in the

form of investments in failed ventures.[2] But compared to
alternative forms of social organization the market process is
an efficient information processor through feedback mechanisms that do not depend on explicit knowledge of the
unknowable.]

In a similar vein, an efficient regulatory scheme to control
the discharge of pollution into the nation's waterways requires
that regulatory authorities know the production function, the
range of technologies for pollution control, and the demand
curves of every major polluter. The alternative approach of
making pollution expensive to create, by levying a charge on
each unit of effluent discharged, sets in motion the informa-
tion-processing and feedback mechanism of the market. In
order to maximize profits, or at a minimum to avoid ultimate
failure, individual polluting firms would have to grope toward
a least-cost approach to pollution control. The knowledge required of the pollution-control authorities, while still formidable, is sharply lessened under the effluent-charge approach.

The more complicated and extensive the social intervention,
and the more it seeks to alter individual behavior, the more
difficult it becomes to accumulate the necessary information
at a central level. It is relatively easy to set up a system of
payroll records from which to determine social security benefits. Doing something about the delivery structure of medical
care or controlling industrial accidents imposes informational
requirements of a much higher order. Obviously, one does not
rush out, on the basis of informational economies alone, and
recommend that education be turned over to the private market and sold like toothpaste, or that simple effluent charges
displace all pollution-control regulations. But, where feasible,
building some freedom of choice into social programs does

2. Where very large forward commitments are required, and in the
case of exhaustible natural resources, the fact that extensive futures and
insurance markets cannot be established may lead to very large inefficiencies. Kenneth J. Arrow, "Limited Knowledge and Economic Analysis,"
American Economic Review, vol. 64 (March 1974), pp. 1–10.

offer advantages, either in generating explicit information for policymakers about the desirability of alternative outcomes or in bypassing the need for certain types of information altogether.

3. A third advantage of the market as a means of social organization is its "devil take the hindmost" approach to questions of individual equity. At first blush this is an outrageous statement, worthy of the coldest heart among last century's Benthamites. And, obviously, I have stated the point in a way designed more to catch the eye than to be precise.

To elaborate, in any except a completely stagnant society, an efficient use of resources means constant change. From the standpoint of static efficiency the more completely and rapidly the economy shifts production to meet changes in consumer tastes, production technologies, resource availability, or locational advantages, the greater the efficiency. From a dynamic standpoint the greater the advances in technology and the faster they are adopted, the greater the efficiency. While these changes on balance generate gains for society in the form of higher living standards, almost every one of them deprives some firms and individuals of income, often temporarily and for only a few, but sometimes permanently and for large numbers. The introduction of a new technology in a firm may displace a handful of skilled workers who, after a period of unemployment, find equivalent jobs elsewhere. Or a shoe factory in a one-plant community may close, permanently lowering the income of middle-aged skilled workers, local merchants, and property owners. Both of these types of income losses may occur in an economy running at full employment; both are even greater in a recession.[3] Under the social arrangements of

3. The emphasis in this section on losses may seem to contradict the argument advanced earlier that transactions in a market system are a form of unanimous-consent arrangement in which *each* transaction involves gains for both parties. But the two propositions are consistent. The original employment "contract" between a firm and a worker, voluntarily entered into, did not bind the firm to keep the worker on the payroll forever, nor did the worker indenture himself forever. Obviously, each would

the private market, those who may suffer losses are not usually able to stand in the way of change. As a consequence efficiency-creating changes are not seriously impeded.[4] There are three ways in which society can deal with these income losses: (1) prevent the particular changes from taking place, thereby mooting the question; (2) make it up to the losers either with monetary payments (compensation)[5] or with offsetting changes that improve their welfare (logrolling); (3) rather than compensate for each change, use the tax-and-transfer system to ensure that the cumulative effect of all the changes is an income distribution that meets society's standards of fairness and equity.

Each one of these ways of dealing with losses has its own advantages and disadvantages. I shall have to come back to this set of issues several times, since the problem of losses critically influences collective decisions about efficiency. At this point, however, I want to stress one aspect of the loss problem. The standards and values that our society employs when dealing with losses associated with market efficiency are

---

have preferred an arrangement under which only he could terminate the employment. But under all but the most extraordinary circumstances, a *mutually advantageous* employment contract will have a finite term. Precisely because it is a changing world, mutually advantageous contracts cannot be drawn to prevent losses (although they can sometimes be drawn to share losses—whence insurance).

4. This is clearly an overstatement. Through various noncompetitive arrangements firms can and do sometimes slow the adoption of innovations that might cause them losses. Nevertheless, taken as a whole, the market does continually make efficiency-creating moves despite the consequent income losses for some individuals and firms.

5. An efficient move is, by definition, one in which gains exceed losses. Hence, in principle, the payment of full compensation for losses could ensure that at least some were better off and none worse off after the move. There is a large literature qualifying and elaborating this proposition. See Nicholas Kaldor, "Welfare Propositions of Economics and Interpersonal Comparisons of Utility," *Economic Journal*, vol. 49 (September 1939), pp. 549–52; J. R. Hicks, "The Foundations of Welfare Economics," ibid., pp. 696–712; T. de Scitovszky, "A Note on Welfare Propositions in Economics," *Review of Economic Studies*, vol. 9 (1941–1942), pp. 77–88; Frank I. Michelman, "Property, Utility, and Fairness: Comments on the Ethical Foundations of 'Just Compensation' Law," *Harvard Law Review*, vol. 80 (April 1967), pp. 1165–1258.

substantially different from those it uses when faced with the possibility of losses through government actions. In particular, we are chary in dealing with losses by preventing efficiency-creating moves in the marketplace (method 1) but very prone to use this technique in connection with collective actions.

Over the years the American political system has developed a set of formal and informal rules about losses associated with political decisions. First, we tend to subject political decisions to the rule, "Do no direct harm." We can let harms occur as the second- and third-order consequences of political action or through sheer inaction, but we cannot be seen to cause harm to anyone as the direct consequence of collective actions. The rule is far from absolute, and exceptions abound. But it does strongly influence policy. Its specific application is handled, in a limited sphere of cases, by monetary compensations—for example, in condemning private property for a highway. Unemployment compensation is another example of payments made to offset the direct or indirect harms government may inflict.[6] But usually the prevention of loss is sought by designing collective action to avoid it in the first place.

The political system enforces the "do no direct harm" rule by very loose arrangements, in which the effective vote of a particular group on a particular issue is weighted according to the potential harm that a decision might inflict on it. Farmers have much greater weight on the House and Senate Agriculture Committees than on the Education and Labor Committees; the voice of educators is assigned far greater importance on the Education and Labor Committees than on the Aeronautical and Space Sciences Committee. Even after the easing of the cloture rules in the Senate, the legislative process is structured to increase the difficulty of passing legislation in proportion to the size of the harm it may do to a particular group. As a consequence, concentrated large harms to a small group are assigned more weight in the benefit-cost calculus of

6. See Michelman, "Property, Utility, and Fairness," for a statement and critique of the legal status of such compensation rules.

politics than are small harms to large groups: legislation promising small benefits to very large numbers is exceedingly difficult to enact if it results in large harms to very small numbers.

To a point, these implicit rules of the game make sense.
Precisely because government has coercive power, unweighted
majoritarian voting could lead to both gross inefficiencies and
gross inequities.[7] And another way to state the principle of
diminishing marginal utility is to call it the principle of increasing marginal harm: large costs to a few are more to be
avoided than small costs to many. On the other hand, because
the direct harm is minimized, not by compensation arrangements or by general income-redistribution techniques but by
placing limitations on the nature of the collective action, the
overall efficiency of collective action is sharply reduced. Once
put into effect, programs can seldom be eliminated. The regulation of the transportation industry has spawned a set of arrangements whereby the government protects the turf of
railroads from invasion by trucking firms and vice versa and
ensures that existing trucking firms suffer little competition
from new entrants or from contract carriers.[8]

Dealing with the problem of losses, which an emphasis on
efficiency necessarily raises, is one of the stickiest social issues.
There is absolutely nothing in either economic or political
theory to argue that efficiency considerations should always
take precedence. And sometimes there is no way to avoid un-

---

7. A measure whose overall social benefits were lower than its costs
could command passage so long as it were constructed to provide more
benefits than costs to a majority coalition. See James M. Buchanan,
"Simple Majority Voting, Game Theory, and Resource Use," *Canadian
Journal of Economics and Political Science*, vol. 27 (August 1961), pp.
337–48.

8. In the process incredibly absurd prohibitions against potentially
efficient use of trucks have been developed. In many cases truck routes are
required to be circuitous, empty backhauls are imposed, and innovative
cost-cutting arrangements between shipper and carrier are forbidden. Such
absurdities are often denounced as the result of the regulatees capturing
the regulators. In fact, they exemplify the consequences of the "do no
direct harm" rule carried to its full conclusion (after eighty-nine years of
application).

consciionably large losses to some group except by avoiding or
at least moderating changes otherwise called for by efficiency
considerations. Nevertheless, in designing instruments for collective intervention that will avoid loss, we place far too much
stress on eschewing efficient solutions, and far too little on
compensation and general income-redistribution measures.
Over time, the cumulative consequences are likely to be a
much smaller social pie for everyone. How we might improve
the tradeoff between efficiency and income preservation in the
process of social intervention will be one of the topics of the
final chapter.

4. The final virtue of market-like arrangements that I wish to
stress is their potential ability to direct innovation into socially
desirable directions. While the formal economic theory of the
market emphasizes its static-efficiency characteristics—its ability to get the most out of existing resources and technology—
what is far more important is its apparent capacity to stimulate
and take advantage of advancing technology. Living standards
in modern Western countries are, by orders of magnitude,
superior to those of the early seventeenth century. Had the
triumph of the market meant only a more efficient use of the
technologies and resources then available, the gains in living
standards would have been minuscule by comparison. What
made the difference was the stimulation and harnessing of
new technologies and resources. ("Nature" put aluminum,
petroleum, and uranium in the earth's crust; but it took new
technology to make them resources.)

It is not simply that market incentives and the price system
stimulate new technologies in general, but that they tend to
direct invention toward conserving those resources that are
scarce. Agricultural technology for grain production in the
United States developed in the direction of using much land
(which was abundant) and little labor (which was scarce). It
developed differently in Europe and Japan, where land is far
less plentiful relative to labor. More generally, most economic
analyses of the nature of inventions suggest that they tended

to occur in very rough conformity with economic needs and scarcities as signaled by prices and profitability.[9] The corollary to these propositions is that where prices give the wrong signal—that is, do not reflect true economic scarcity—technology responds (or fails to respond) accordingly. Pollution is a classic case. For hundreds of years environmental quality was treated as a free resource. The market responded with marvelous efficiency to that signal and proceeded to develop technology that made maximum use of the air and water as "free" sinks for waste products, and neglected the development of technologies that reduced pollution per unit of output. Automobile engines were designed for speed, acceleration, and low production costs to the accompaniment of smog-creating emissions. Steel mills, coking plants, and paper mills were built to economize on labor and other costs, while using, and fouling, incredible volumes of air and water. Another resource—labor—offers a sharp contrast: it is expensive, and business firms must pay for it, at ever-increasing real wages; as a consequence, over the last century, the amount of labor per unit of output has been halved every thirty years.

From a long-range standpoint, the effectiveness of social intervention in a number of important areas depends critically on heeding this lesson. Much of the economic literature on pollution control, for example, stresses the role of economic incentives to achieve static efficiency in control measures—that is, the use of existing technology in a way that reaches environmental goals at least cost. In the long run, however, the future of society is going to hinge on the discovery and adoption of ever-improving technologies to reduce the environmental consequences of expanding production. If, for example, we assume that per capita living standards in the United States improve from now on at only one-half the rate of the past century, the gross national product a hundred years

9. Jacob Schmookler, *Invention and Economic Growth* (Harvard University Press, 1966); Vernon W. Ruttan, "Research on the Economics of Technological Change in American Agriculture," *Journal of Farm Economics*, vol. 42 (November 1960), pp. 735–54.

from now will still have risen more than threefold. Median family income, now about $14,000, will equal about $55,000. Only if the amount of pollution per unit of output is cut by two-thirds can we maintain current environmental performance, let alone improve it—even on the assumption that the rate of economic growth is halved. There is simply no way such reductions can be achieved unless the direction of technological change is shifted to minimize pollution. It is not a question of one or two dramatic breakthroughs any more than it was in the steady historical reduction of unit labor requirements. The problem of environmental quality permeates most of the production and consumption aspects of the economy. Hence the discovery and adoption of pollution-reducing technology will have to be equally pervasive. Unlike the space program or the Manhattan project, these are not tasks that central direction can accomplish well. Instead, the institutions and incentives of society have to be modified for a steady long-run effort. Reducing pollution has to become a paying proposition rather than just another battle against the regulators.[10]

Congestion in central cities, chemical threats to health, sharply rising medical costs, and the pressure of economic growth on scarce natural resources are other areas in which society already has intervened and in which the avoidance of long-term problems depends especially on the response of technology to social needs. The point is not that the unfettered market can deal with these problems. Indeed, the problems arise precisely because the market as it is now structured does not work well. But the historically demonstrated power of market-like incentives to influence the pace and direction of technological change warrants every effort to install such incentives in our programs of social intervention.

10. For a more specific statement of why current pollution-control programs may actually hinder the long-run development of technology, see Henry D. Jacoby, John D. Steinbruner, and others, *Clearing the Air: Federal Policy in Automotive Emissions Control* (Ballinger, 1973); Allen V. Kneese and Charles L. Schultze, *Pollution, Prices, and Public Policy* (Brookings Institution, 1975), pp. 112–13.

III

ALTHOUGH market-like arrangements have strategic advantages for organizing a broad range of human activities, that range is not all-encompassing. There is virtually unanimous agreement that basic human and political rights should not be bought and sold, and that relationships within the family should not be governed by the calculus of dollars. Similarly, some aspects of education and, more recently, of health care have been partly insulated from the market. We exclude many areas from the market not because it is inefficient, but because of fundamental considerations of liberty and human dignity. Arthur Okun covered this ground in his Godkin Lectures two years ago and I do not intend to pursue the point, except when it unavoidably intrudes.

Within the sphere of activities not excluded from the market by considerations of liberty and dignity, there remain many situations in which private enterprise operating in a free market as we now know it does not produce efficient results. Where the deviations are serious, a prima facie case arises for collective intervention on grounds of efficiency alone. Paradoxically, most of these situations occur where private enterprise itself does not make a proper market for some important output or input.

Where the market process fails, too much or too little of some output will be produced. We get too little environmental quality, or too many industrial accidents, or too much traffic congestion. Society can go about dealing with market failure in two quite different ways. It can try to isolate the causes of the failure and restore, as nearly as possible, an efficient market process. Or it can put matters completely into governmental hands, supplant the market, and directly determine the outputs it wants. In other words, social intervention can be *process-oriented*, seeking to correct the faulty process, or *output-oriented*, seeking to bypass the process and determine outputs directly by regulation or other device.

Neither approach is universally valid. In some circumstances the obstacles to creating a working market process are insuperable. But in many cases, corrective action to create efficient markets is possible. Regardless of the circumstances, however, social intervention has almost always been output-oriented, giving short shrift to the process-oriented alternative. And this has proven a costly bias. It has, with no offsetting gain, forfeited the strategic advantages of market-like arrangements. It has led to ineffective and inefficient solutions to important social problems. It has taxed, well beyond its limit, the ability of government to make complex output decisions. And it has stretched thin the delicate fabric of political consensus by unnecessarily widening the scope of activities it must cover.

Documenting this thesis is the task of this chapter. It starts with a brief explanation of the generic causes of market failure —the circumstances under which unaided private markets are unlikely to be efficient. It then takes up specific cases of market failure, examining the output-oriented techniques that social intervention now employs, and contrasting them with alternatives that seek to modify and correct the root causes of market failure rather than replace the market process.

THE CAUSES OF MARKET FAILURE

Any consideration of the causes of market failure must start with the fact that there exists no such animal as a "natural" laissez-faire system sprung solely from private arrangements. I cannot buy and you cannot sell until both of us know what is mine and what is yours. Before trade can occur, there must be an underlying social agreement to define, and enforce, property rights. The agreement may be simply to respect some cus-

tomary practices. But every modern society is based upon a
set of property laws that specify, either in legislation or by
judicial precedent, a highly complex set of dos and don'ts,
liabilities and privileges, with respect to owning, using, buying,
and selling property.[1]

The structure of the private enterprise system and the efficiency with which it operates depend on the content of this
system of property and contract laws. Patent laws turn some
forms of human knowledge into salable property, and strongly
influence the pace of technological progress and the structure
of industry. Because until recently the law did not assign property rights in the assimilative capacity of the air and water,
anyone could use them free of charge as dumps for waste, and
so everyone did—to excess. Legal assignment of liability to
physicians for certain kinds of medical damage and the easing
of standards of proof for negligence in medical malpractice
suits have substantially affected the way in which medicine is
practiced.

The free enterprise system, therefore, carries the label
"made by government." How efficiently that system works at
any point in time is strongly conditioned by how well the
structure of property laws matches the underlying technological and economic realities. If those realities change, and property laws do not, there is bound to be trouble.[2]

A second basic proposition underlies an identification and
analysis of market failure: to be an efficient instrument for
society a private market must be so organized that buyers and

1. This includes socialist societies. Their definitions of property are
as complex as those in capitalist societies.
2. In the past decade research and theoretical development in the
"economics of the law" have mushroomed. See, for example, A. Mitchell
Polinsky, "Economic Analysis as a Potentially Defective Product: A
Buyer's Guide to Posner's Economic Analysis of Law," *Harvard Law
Review*, vol. 87 (June 1974), pp. 1655–81; Guido Calabresi, "Transaction Costs, Resource Allocation and Liability Rules—A Comment,"
Journal of Law and Economics, vol. 11 (April 1968), pp. 67–73; R. H.
Coase, "The Problem of Social Cost," ibid., vol. 3 (October 1960), pp.
1–44; Richard A. Posner, *Economic Analysis of Law* (Little, Brown,
1972).

extrernalities

sellers realize *all* the benefits and pay *all* the costs of each transaction. In other words, the price paid by the buyer and the costs incurred by the seller in each private transaction must reflect the full value and the full cost of that transaction not only to them, but to society as a whole. My decision to drive to work will reflect my own balancing of the benefits I receive from auto transportation against the money and time costs I thereby incur. But if streets are already congested, the addition of my car to the traffic will lengthen the time it takes everyone else to commute and impose real costs on society that I did not take into account in my own decision. There will be more auto commuting than is truly efficient.

As a rough and ready generalization, the body of laws governing property rights and liabilities is likely to yield inefficient results principally when dealing with the side effects of private market transactions. The problem is not that side effects exist, but that the benefits they confer or the costs they impose are often not reflected in the prices and costs that guide private decisions. Sometimes the side effects are confined to the parties making the transaction, as in many cases of defects in consumer products or job-related injuries. But often the side effects impose costs (or confer benefits) on large numbers of people who were not parties to the transaction. Air and water pollution from industrial activity cause damage over wide areas to people who had no part in the production or purchase of the goods being produced. Auto commuters on congested streets create traffic delays for each other with no transactions involved. To the extent that an educated population makes for a better citizenry, my decision to send my children to college generates socially beneficial side effects to the whole population.[3]

3. Opposing views are expressed in Paul Taubman and Terence Wales, *Higher Education and Earnings* (McGraw-Hill, 1974), in which education is seen as a screening device; and in Richard B. Freeman, "Overinvestment in College Training?" *Journal of Human Resources*, vol. 10 (Summer 1975), pp. 287–311, which presents evidence of an overinvestment in college training.

Where side effects are confined to the parties to a transaction, proper specification of the laws governing private property can sometimes ensure that they are properly reflected in
the private accounting of costs and benefits. Under these circumstances, establishing some continuing mechanism of social
intervention is unnecessary. Individual buy-and-sell arrangements can efficiently reflect social values. The introduction of
workmen's compensation laws, for example, shifted the prima
facie liability for work-related injuries to employers—that is,
the injured worker did not have to prove negligence in court in
order to collect damages. The intent of the shift was to make
it more probable that employers would face the true social
costs of their choices about how to organize production, and
thus, for the sake of increasing their own profits, act to reduce
such costs.[4]

In many cases, however, the very nature of the situation is
such that merely redefining property rights will not resolve the
problem; markets can be organized by purely private efforts
only at great cost, if at all. This is sometimes true even when
the side effects are confined to the parties making a transaction,
as in the case of work-related injuries. It is almost universally
true when many other parties are involved.

There are essentially four sets of factors whose existence
leads to market failure and also limits the range of corrective
action available to society: high transaction costs; large uncertainty; high information costs; and finally, what economists
call the "free rider" problem. They are often present in
combination.

Transaction Costs

Markets are not costless. There are expenses of money,
time, and effort in setting and collecting prices. Sometimes

4. This is a highly truncated statement of a complicated issue. The
problem of occupational safety and health is discussed in greater detail
below.

transaction costs are virtually infinite: there is no conceivable way that a market can be formed to deal with side effects. Sometimes transaction costs, while not infinite, exceed the benefits that a market could otherwise confer, and so it doesn't pay to set one up. Very often the scope and nature of the transaction costs strongly limit the range of effective social intervention, and force society to organize markets in less than an ideal way.

Traffic congestion provides a good example of all of these situations. The decisions of individual drivers to commute through crowded downtown streets create costly side effects; each decision to drive imposes costs in delay on other drivers. Could the law be changed to create property rights in the side effects? Could I be forced to buy "rights" to drive from other drivers on whom my decisions would impose delay? Obviously not. There is no conceivable way in which the tens of thousands of drivers could calculate the myriad bids and offers, transfer net balances of payments, and monitor and enforce agreements. Could local governments establish a quasi-market —set up a schedule of congestion tolls and charge each driver according to the time of day and the degree of congestion along the particular streets he travels? While ingenious schemes have been suggested,[5] involving radar and computerized billing, the costs of setting up such quasi-markets seem to rule them out. What about stiff parking fees downtown, or the sale by government of monthly downtown auto permits? Those who value their daily auto trip highly would be willing to pay, others would use mass transit, and congestion could be reduced for both groups. The transaction costs of such a scheme would be much lower, but the prices charged would

5. See William Vickrey, "Pricing as a Tool in Coordination of Local Transportation," in *Transportation Economics*, A Conference of the Universities-National Bureau Committee for Economic Research (Columbia University Press for the National Bureau of Economic Research, 1965); and *Road Pricing: The Economic and Technical Possibilities*, Report of a Panel set up by the Ministry of Transport (London: Her Majesty's Stationery Office, 1964).

lose some of their relationship to the particular circumstances causing congestion. My contribution to congestion varies according to when I drive and along what streets, but the parking fee or commuting permit charges me a price that is only the roughest approximation to that contribution. Hence, the resulting scheme will not be ideally efficient. Nevertheless, it may lead to a more efficient result than the two polar opposites—doing nothing, or forbidding the use of certain areas to private automobiles.

A program recently implemented in Singapore has been very successful in reducing traffic. Under that program, motorists in cars carrying fewer than four people must buy licenses to enter the central business district during the morning rush hour. Supplementing this scheme is a system of high inner-city parking rates, expanded peripheral parking facilities, and improved mass transportation. Initial results indicate that congestion in the business district has been reduced by 40 percent as a result of this innovation.[6]

Dealing with environmental damages is beset with problems of transaction costs. For example, a simple redefinition of property laws obviously cannot create a market in salable rights to emit auto exhausts. Ideally, an efficient quasi-market might be created if society levied a fee (that is, charged a price) on driving scaled to match the exhaust damages generated thereby. But the damages caused by auto exhausts vary with the type of automobile, the nature of the driving, the region of the country, and atmospheric conditions. To calculate and collect such a sophisticated set of fees would be tremendously costly and inconvenient. The question then arises, is it more efficient to levy a simplified set of emission fees (based on the average emissions of an automobile and perhaps accompanied by a new tax on gasoline) which matches damages only imperfectly? Or should we give up on the market completely and

6. Peter L. Watson and Edward P. Holland, "Congestion Pricing—the Example of Singapore," *Finance and Development*, vol. 13 (March 1976), pp. 20–23.

promulgate regulations on new cars that specify emission limits?

Setting prices on harmful side effects is the most desirable means of reducing them when a large number of technically feasible ways exist to accomplish reductions and a continuous range of adjustment is possible. As more and more wastes containing BOD (biochemical oxygen demand) are dumped into a river, the damage to fish and wildlife and to human uses gradually increases.[7] Levying a stiff fee on each pound of BOD discharged would induce each polluter to seek out the least costly ways of reducing his discharges. Polluters themselves would have an incentive to find better and cheaper ways to reduce damages. Moreover, those with the lowest costs of reduction would cut back by more than those with the highest costs, and the desired standard of water quality would thereby tend to be reached at lowest cost. In the case of very toxic chemicals, such as Kepone or dieldrin, however, very small amounts can cause very great damage. The amounts entering the environment have to be severely limited, if not cut to zero. Unlike the case of BOD, there is no efficiency gain in having producers facing different costs cut back by different amounts. In theory one could extend the market mechanism to this case, too: the charge levied on the discharge of each unit of toxic chemicals would be so large that no one would discharge any units. But the game isn't worth the candle. When a fairly simple and easily calculable result is wanted, the delicate adjustments that a price system is capable of producing are not relevant. Hence, regulatory limitations or flat prohibition may be the least costly and most effective solution.

Uncertainty and Information Costs

It is easier to treat the problems of uncertainty and information costs together since it is through information that we can,

---

7. There is a lower threshold below which damages are virtually zero and an upper threshold beyond which the containing water becomes anaerobic.

at least sometimes, reduce uncertainty. Market transactions cannot be an efficient method of organizing human activity unless both the buyer and the seller understand the full costs and benefits to them of the transactions they undertake, including any side effects that impinge on their own welfare. If, for example, the legal principle of caveat emptor prevails, consumers are responsible for judging the reliability and safety of the products they buy. If, at reasonable costs in time, money, and mental effort, they can acquire and interpret information about the quality of products, then safer and more reliable brands will command a premium over dangerous and less reliable products. The premium will reflect judgments by consumers about the value to them of safety and reliability. Producers in turn will find it profitable to push safety and reliability up to the point at which the costs of doing so begin to exceed the premium; in short, an efficient outcome will be assured. On similar reasoning, workers will evaluate the risks of injury in various jobs; dangerous jobs will command a wage premium; and employers will have an incentive to pursue injury-avoiding measures in order to reduce the premium. (With the enactment of workmen's compensation laws, liability for work-related accidents was, in part at least, shifted to employers, who then faced the cost of work-related injuries, not in wage premiums but in premiums for workmen's compensation insurance.)

One concomitant of growing affluence has been the introduction of complex and potentially dangerous consumer products—power tools, power lawnmowers, microwave ovens, powerful drugs, and so forth. In making a one-time purchase of such items the individual consumer is hard put to acquire and interpret information about their safety characteristics. The experiences of friends and neighbors are helpful but such anecdotal evidence is likely to be imperfect or misleading. Although commercial testing firms conceivably could fill this gap, there is an inherent limitation to the efficiency of developing and disseminating information on consumer products in this way. The overhead costs of buying and testing consumer products in sufficient numbers to give reliable results are quite large. Models proliferate and are likely to be changed frequently. As a consequence, the subscription price that a private testing firm has to charge to cover the costs of its services is apt to be so high as to discourage its widespread use.[8] Government-sponsored research and testing, or labeling requirements, may be needed to overcome the high costs of information.

The public provision of consumer information sometimes poses a dilemma. In the case of hazards that are highly complicated, the provision of technically complete but neutral information may not be very helpful. Evaluating the significance of the hazard on the basis of new information may itself require more technical ability and judgment and more time than it is reasonable to expect from most consumers. Alternatively, government can regulate the safety characteristics of such products, almost always pushing the price up. And in some cases a ban on certain types of products may be imposed, which is equivalent to charging an infinitely high price. In such situations the single risk evaluation of a governmental body is substituted for the diverse judgments of millions of consumers, some of whom may have preferred a lower price and more risk to a higher price and less risk.

The temptation to overregulate is great, and should be resisted. Quite apart from safety features, there are a host of product characteristics—performance, reliability, durability— that often depend upon highly technical factors. The usual consumer information about such characteristics is casual and imperfect, and in the case of durable goods information cannot be gathered by trial and error. Market demand and price dif-

8. Technically, producing consumer-product information is a decreasing-cost industry. The marginal costs of disseminating the information to additional consumers are less than average costs (including the testing). A private firm charging a socially efficient price to consumers would not be able to cover all its costs. Hence, from society's standpoint, the private market will produce too little consumer information.

ferentials among products therefore do not reflect evaluations based on perfect information. If the mere existence of market imperfection is allowed to become the occasion for regulation, society would have to regulate every characteristic of every durable product. But the benefits of potentially superior information that a regulator can bring to bear have to be balanced against the inability of monolithic regulatory judgments to match the diverse preferences of individuals and against the inevitable sluggishness with which regulators adapt to changing circumstances. Where the potential harms from a product feature are serious and where the technical difficulty of evaluating information is very great, regulation may be the best alternative despite its inefficiencies. But in all cases the comparison should be between an imperfect market and an imperfect regulatory scheme, not some ideal abstraction.

Uncertainty and information costs impede the ability of market transactions to yield desirable results in the case of occupational health hazards. Usually injuries at the workplace are easily detectable and liability under workmen's compensation laws is easily assignable. The social costs of the injuries are borne by the employer, and the appropriate incentives for minimizing injury are present.[9] But the more subtle threats to health from exotic chemicals, cancer-inducing agents like asbestos, and similar causes, pose almost insuperable difficulties that cannot be handled under the normal legal rules for assignment of liability. (And these kinds of dangers steadily increase in a technological society.) In the first place, the private market offers no incentives to undertake the research necessary to pinpoint the health hazards from particular production processes. Second, the nature of the hazards is inherently probabilistic. Spending twenty-five years exposed to asbestos fibers at

9. Legal limits on the size of awards, however, sometimes result in the costs to the employer being lower than the damage suffered by an injured worker. See Nina W. Cornell, Roger G. Noll, and Barry Weingast, "Safety Regulation," in Henry Owen and Charles L. Schultze, eds., *Setting National Priorities: The Next Ten Years* (Brookings Institution, 1976), pp. 457–504.

the workplace, for example, might raise the probability of lung cancer from 0.03 to 0.04, an increase of 33 percent. Ideally, to provide the appropriate incentives for reducing this risk, the employer should be liable to pay every worker contracting lung cancer one-quarter the value of the damages thereby incurred. But in the courts one is either liable or not liable. Legal findings of liability are not suited to probabilistic situations. Moreover, even the probabilities are highly uncertain in most cases, since different studies of the causal connections between chemical exposure and bad health typically estimate different probabilities of incidence, and sometimes disagree about the very existence of a connection. Given the usual judicial rules of evidence, sustaining liability in these kinds of situations is virtually impossible. There is no practical way, therefore, for the market to price such subtle and uncertain side effects, or even for government to create a quasi-market by assigning prices. Government research and regulation of health-related working conditions are needed. Research can reduce the uncertainty, but much will remain. In the face of large and ineradicable uncertainty no precise benefit-cost calculus can be applied either by the market or by the regulators. Ultimately, the stringency of regulations, and the size of the economic costs they impose, must depend upon a judgmental assessment of risks. Over time, continued research can usually be expected to reduce the range of uncertainty. In the interim, it would be wise to build conservative safety margins into the regulations in those cases in which fatal or disabling consequences are suspected.

High information costs and large uncertainty can also impede the efficiency of market transactions when individuals or firms confront heavy long-term investments. An individual private decisionmaker may be reluctant to undertake a worthwhile but risky investment if the potential losses of guessing wrong about the future are very high relative to his income and financial assets. Society as a whole, through government, can pool the risks from many different investments; losses from a few bad guesses can be averaged in with the gains from others.

Without arguing the case, I shall assert that this possibility provides no warrant for direct government investment or government guarantees in the normal run of business activities. The possible gains from a lower risk premium are swamped by the disadvantages of transferring business investment decisions to a bureaucratic framework. But three major exceptions stand out.

Education is an investment in human capital. On the average it pays a good return. Studies show that the rate of return on higher education, for example, compares favorably with that on business investment. But the range of possible outcomes is very wide. The return to any one individual depends on a combination of luck, ability, and motivation. And the investment required for college or more advanced education is very large compared with the income and financial assets of the average family—let alone the poor. Unlike investments in business plant and equipment or home construction, no salable assets result from educational investments that can be pledged as collateral for a loan; we do not allow slavery or indentured services. In any given case, the risk of such an investment is therefore very great as seen both by a potential lender and by the family of the potential student. Again, the poorer the family, the greater the risk; thus, the less the likelihood that educational investments, which in the aggregate would pay off, will be made. For reasons of both equality of opportunity and efficiency, government has a role in underwriting some of the risk.[10]

In theory, at least, potentially dynamic and innovative small businesses seeking to finance risky investments may suffer from the same kind of imperfections in the capital market.[11] Often

10. Merely guaranteeing educational loans will not be sufficient. This eliminates the risk to the lender but not to the borrower (unless the loan is a subterfuge for a grant, in the sense that no one attempts to collect it)

11. A risky investment is *not* one that can be expected to fail. Rather, it is one in which there is great uncertainty about the payoff. A risky investment might, as a best estimate, be expected to yield a very good return of 20 percent, but with a 30 percent probability of yielding upward of 40 percent and a 30 percent probability of suffering a loss.

the capital needed to carry out some new idea is very large compared with current income and assets and they have neither the prior history of good earnings nor the long association with particular lenders that helps bigger and older firms secure capital on reasonable terms. Conceptually, at least, this problem could be eased by social intervention to increase the flow of risk capital to promising but risky small-business investment. In fact, as I shall point out below, the current small-business program of the federal government bears little relation to the nature of the market failure it is supposed to correct.

Finally, there are occasions when uncertainties about the future are so great, and investment requirements so large, that even sizable and well-established business firms may be unwilling to undertake ventures that, from society's standpoint, are desirable. Large-scale investment in newer forms of energy —synthetic-fuel plants, for example—may be held up, not principally because of the newness of the processes, but because of the uncertain prospect for oil prices. The cost of extracting and delivering Middle East oil to the United States is in the neighborhood of $2 a barrel; the current price is about $14. If cutting prices is necessary to preserve markets, the cartel operated by the Organization of Petroleum Exporting Countries has ample room to do so while still realizing handsome profits. Even if a reasonable return could be earned on a twenty-five-year investment with a $14 market price for synthetic fuels, the huge gap between costs and prices for most OPEC oil poses the kind of uncertainty with which even large private firms find it difficult to live. If investment in synthetic fuels is deemed desirable, some form of risk assumption by government will probably be necessary. Unless the particular form is matched to the nature of the risk, however, the results are likely to be poor. The unusual risk in this case is a *price* risk; guaranteeing a minimum price for the output of specific plants would make sense. The normal incentives for minimization of costs would remain. Guaranteeing loans for synthetic-fuel investments would not make sense, since the venture would be bailed out even if the failure stemmed from bad management rather than OPEC price cutting.

The "Free Rider" Problem

Where the side effects of private transactions have a common impact on many people—for example, in the discharge of sulfur into the atmosphere from coal-burning utilities—the possibility of purely private action is severely limited. In theory, if the rights to the use of the clean air were assigned by law to the polluter, those affected might band together and pay the polluter to reduce the emissions. But any one individual would enjoy the benefits of the improvement whether he paid his share of the cost or not. He could be a "free rider" on the efforts of everyone else. How could cost shares be decided and enforced? Without the coercive power of government, purely voluntary arrangements could not be successful. Conversely, if the rights were assigned to those affected by pollution so that the polluter had to buy rights to emit sulfur, how would agreement be reached on the appropriate payment and the sharing out of the proceeds? Purely voluntary action implies unanimous consent.

We do undertake some actions of this nature by unanimous-consent arrangements. The implicit neighborhood agreement that no one mows the lawn on Sunday morning is one such. But as a means of dealing with important and widespread side effects of private transactions, voluntary arrangements would quickly break down.[12]

For formal completeness, I should note that it is the combination of high transactions cost and free-rider problems that makes it necessary for government itself to arrange for the

---

12. In addition, the transaction costs of negotiating purely private arrangements, even without the free-rider problem, would often prove prohibitive.

production of certain kinds of goods and services—what the economist calls "public goods." National defense and police protection, for example, cannot be bought and sold in the private market. Their benefits are commonly available to everyone. Under purely voluntary arrangements there would be no incentive for any one individual to pay his share of costs, since he would receive the benefits anyway.

Market Failure in a Federal System of Government

In a government like ours, arranged in a federal system, a unique allocation of responsibilities among federal, state, and local governments would be inefficient for reasons closely analogous to those that cause market failure in the private sector. We cannot say, for example, that financing education and social services should be assigned solely to local governments, highways and control of water pollution to state governments alone, and flood control to the federal government. Quite apart from fairness and equity, which might warrant some form of general revenue sharing, efficiency argues for certain types of joint action and joint financing by several levels of government. I would like to concentrate on the role of the federal government in this context.

Just as they do in the case of private market transactions, side effects and spillovers arise from the tax and spending decisions of state and local governments; the benefits and costs of particular actions sometimes extend beyond the jurisdiction taking the action. The dumping of raw sewage into a river by an upstream locality ruins the river for those who live downstream. The other side of the coin is that taxes to pay for the construction and operation of waste-treatment plants would have to be borne by the upstream residents for the benefit of those downstream. In theory, a clear definition of "property laws" assigning rights in clean water to the downstream communities would enable them to join together, set a price on the dumping of wastes, and thereby provide incentives to the upstream community to put up a waste-treatment plant.[13] In fact, the nature of the pollution problem along most river basins is so complex, the transaction costs of negotiating efficient arrangements among a host of small communities so high, and the free-rider problem so pervasive, that purely voluntary arrangements are not likely to be effective. Intervention by a higher level of government is necessary. Transportation—investments in highways, mass transit, airports, and other facilities—poses the same kind of problem. In a highly mobile population, the public benefits of educational investments by one community ultimately accrue to many other communities, and failure to devote enough resources to education in one place ultimately penalizes taxpayers in distant places.

The tax and spending decisions reached by state and local governments have benefits and costs that extend beyond their own boundaries; but since they are made solely in the interests of their own citizens, they may not give efficient results from a national standpoint. Much of the benefits and costs of such actions, however, still are confined to the decisionmaking jurisdictions. Local needs and preferences legitimately differ. Hence, dealing with the side effects of state and local decisions by substituting the purely centralized decisions of the federal government would introduce the opposite kind of inefficiency. Centralized decisionmaking necessarily homogenizes local differences in needs and preferences, and so also fails the test of efficiency. The system of categorical grants-in-aid has become the means of trying to reconcile the two objectives, allowing some diversity in state and local provision of services but supplementing those levels to take account of nationally significant side effects. As in the case of federal intervention in the private sector, however, this system has developed in a way that often bears little relation to the underlying "market" failure, a problem to which I shall return.

13. Even if the property laws conferred the rights to the use of the waterway upon the polluter, the downstream communities could, in theory, band together and "bribe" the upstream community to reduce pollution.

There are several other sources of market failure in the federal system. Reasonably equitable treatment of the poor and the disadvantaged involves not only the distribution of income, but also a fair share of locally delivered public services. And in the case of some public services, like education and skill training, equality of earning opportunities may require a larger per capita provision for the poor and disadvantaged than for other people. But when it comes to local decisions about such matters, there is an inherent bias in the system. The more a community puts into such services, the higher its tax rates compared to the benefits it provides for middle- and upper-income taxpayers. Leaving basic decisions about these matters to state and local governments is unfair to both their taxpayers and their poor. A voter might be perfectly willing to vote compensatory education or skill training for the poor, but would balk if only his state or community were providing such assistance. States and localities with lower levels of assistance to the poor would have an advantage, via lower tax rates, in attracting industries and well-to-do persons, and thereby lowering tax rates still further. Voting for higher levels of services to the disadvantaged would thus cost the taxpayer in that state twice: first, the direct cost of the program; and second, the indirect cost associated with the worsened competitive position of the state. In effect, the system is inefficient in meeting the needs of equity and equal opportunity. Federal grants are warranted to help equalize the provision of such compensatory services among jurisdictions.

Finally, the development of new institutions and techniques of delivering public services may need assistance. Research, development, and experimentation with potential improvements in the production of locally delivered public services are unlikely to be pressed far by individual jurisdictions, since the costs and risks are locally borne while the benefits from successful innovation are national in scope. The markets for local public services are neither competitive nor national; they are unlike the markets for many private goods, which are national and served by national firms, and in which innovations once

proven tend to spread quickly. Such considerations provide a
rationale for federal grants to initiate new ways of delivering
health care in poor inner-city neighborhoods and rural areas,
for community mental-health centers, and for manpower-
training centers.

PUBLIC FAILURES IN DEALING
WITH MARKET FAILURES

I have examined some of the strategic advantages of the market
of voluntary exchange, and of local governmental decisions, as
a technique for organizing a large sphere of human activity. I
have also tried to look systematically at the circumstances in
which the market on its own fails to produce reasonably efficient results, thereby providing the occasions for social intervention. But as the discussion has suggested in bits and pieces,
the specific forms of social intervention over the years have
often had only a tenuous relation to the particular nature of
the market failures to which they were addressed. Usually,
when a problem has been singled out for public action, little
attempt has been made to isolate the causes of market failure
and deal with them in a way that preserves as many as possible
of the elements of voluntary choice and private incentives.
Rather, intervention typically substitutes a centralized command-and-control approach to decisionmaking over a far
broader area than is necessary to deal with the market failure
in question. It is impossible to provide an overall measurement
of the mismatch between the occasions for intervention and
the forms that intervention has taken. But several broad traits
have characterized public policy: the effort to affect private
activity by regulation, and the effort to influence state and
local governments by detailed grant programs.

Regulation

One broad class of market failure stems from the inability
of the unaided private market to put a price on important side

effects of economic transactions and so to subject them to the efficiency calculus that balances costs against gains. As we saw, given the complicated situations in which many of the side effects occur, changes in property laws are not usually adequate to create an ideal pricing structure for these effects. Hence, in each case, we have to balance the imperfect efficiency of an artificially created pricing structure against the imperfect efficiency of a regulatory or other nonpricing approach. The virtually universal characteristic of public policy in these circumstances is to *start* from the conclusion that regulation is the obvious answer; the pricing alternative is never considered.

Precisely because environmental problems are so pervasive they illustrate the gamut of pricing situations, ranging from those in which environmental side effects can reasonably be priced to those in which information or transaction costs make pricing ineffective or excessively expensive.[14] Effective policy must recognize that almost every industry, and every situation, presents alternative ways to reduce pollution that vary widely in effectiveness and cost. Nationally, the difference between efficient and inefficient control programs can, over a ten-year period, mount into the hundreds of billions of dollars.[15] Policy must also operate in a world of imperfect knowledge in which the relative cost and effectiveness of various abatement techniques and the interaction of pollutants with the environment are subject to great uncertainty. Policy must deal both with situations in which targets and deadlines can and ought to be adjusted depending on costs and other circum-

14. As Kneese and d'Arge have pointed out, the law of conservation of mass guarantees that in all our acts of producing and consuming goods we never destroy matter (except in minutest amounts in nuclear reactions) but return it to the environment. Virtually every economic activity has environmental consequences. See Allen V. Kneese and Ralph C. d'Arge, "Pervasive External Costs and the Response of Society," in *The Analysis and Evaluation of Public Expenditures: The PPB System*, A Compendium of Papers Submitted to the Subcommittee on Economy in Government of the Joint Economic Committee, 91:1 (GPO, 1969), vol: 1, pp. 87–115.

15. Allen V. Kneese and Charles L. Schultze, *Pollution, Prices, and Public Policy* (Brookings Institution, 1975), pp. 69–84.

stances, and with cases of potentially fatal toxic chemicals that offer little if any flexibility. And finally, policy must avoid locking the nation into uniform technological choices that discourage a continuing search for better control methods.

Controlling the emissions of sulfur from the combustion of fossil fuels in electric utilities is a good example, especially in the context of another important national goal, the substitution of coal for oil as a source of energy. Current national policy is based on the 1970 Clean Air Amendments. Under that law the Environmental Protection Agency (EPA) has set threshold values, called primary standards, for the concentration of sulfur oxides in the air. These threshold values are a regulatory fiction: arbitrarily, concentrations above this level are taken to be injurious to human health; lower concentrations are considered harmless. More rigorous "secondary" standards, designed to protect property, crops, livestock, and "the public welfare" from damage, were also established. In 1973, a Supreme Court ruling affirming a lower court decision (*Sierra Club* v. *Ruckelshaus*) compounded the regulatory confusion. It found that the language of the 1970 act also required the prevention of any "significant deterioration" of ambient air quality even in regions whose air quality is above secondary standards.

States have prepared implementation plans detailing specific limitations on SO_2 (sulfur dioxide) emissions from each existing source, including public utilities. Enforceable schedules for complying with these limits are also included in the plans. In conjunction with standards for new sources, the emission limitations and compliance schedules were calculated to meet the primary standards by mid-1975 and the secondary standards several years later while ensuring against significant deterioration of air quality (as defined by the EPA and the states).

In addition, the EPA itself was charged with developing limitations on emissions of newly constructed generating plants and other facilities. The EPA standards serve as an upper limit on emissions from new sources. However, if a state's standard is less stringent than EPA's, enforcement is EPA's responsibility.[16]

New facilities thus have to meet two requirements—they cannot exceed EPA emission limits (or those of the state, whichever are more stringent), and they cannot cause concentrations of sulfur oxides in the atmosphere to increase beyond the national air-quality standards or the deterioration standards.

Low-sulfur coal is scarce and frequently even it cannot meet the standards without further action to remove the sulfur. Up until the 1973 oil embargo, public utilities were moving to meet air-quality standards by switching from coal to low-sulfur oil. But national policy now aims at reversing this trend. Under legislation enacted in 1974 new oil-burning plants are generally prohibited, and the Federal Energy Administration has selected eighty power plants to convert from oil to coal subject to an EPA determination that doing so will not violate air-quality standards.[17] As of September 1976, EPA had approved only thirty-two of the eighty conversions. The principal technique currently available for burning coal while still keeping SO_2 emissions low is the use of "scrubbers," which remove sulfur from the smoke in the smokestack. Scrubbers are very expensive to install and maintain, and themselves use 2 to 5 percent of the energy output of the generating plant. For some time many public utilities were urging an alternative approach—tall smokestacks to disperse SO_2 over a broader area, thereby diluting its concentration, and a system of intermittent controls that would shut down coal burners or switch to low-sulfur fuel when meteorological conditions were adverse. EPA, however, has finally decided to limit sharply the use of tall smokestacks and intermittent controls as a means of complying with air-quality standards.

16. States can set standards for new sources more or less stringent than EPA's.
17. The Energy Supply and Environmental Coordination Act of 1974.

The combination of the 1970 act and the High Court's 1973
decision has resulted in a particularly rigid and unpromising
approach, especially in view of the conflicting goal of oil conservation. Utilities must meet a highly specific emission standard. Unless a proposed scrubber installation fully meets the
standard, a new coal plant cannot go ahead—a miss is as bad
as a mile. Moreover, once the standard has been met no incentive remains for continued improvement.

The nondegradation policy does attempt, in a very inefficient way, to address a real problem. Even when SO_2 is diluted
by dispersion, it eventually falls out of the atmosphere in the
form of harmful sulfates and acid rains which are damaging to
crops and health. Moreover, large-scale air movements spread
this kind of damage all across the country. Hence it is necessary to worry about the cumulative amount of SO_2 put into
the atmosphere even from regions whose air quality is well
above primary and secondary standards.

One way of dealing with many of these rigidities would be
to institute a stiff nationwide tax on each pound of SO_2 dis-
persed into the atmosphere (possibly with an additional charge
during periods of adverse weather conditions). Current primary standards could be maintained, but with the imposition
of the tax, deadlines could be relaxed for secondary standards
and the nondegradation policy eliminated (except for those
specially designated areas, often around national parks, where
very stringent controls are indeed warranted). The fiction that
pollution damages are zero up to a given standard and almost
infinitely high above it—which is implied by the current approach—is not useful. The sulfur tax, on the other hand, would
set up nationwide incentives to reduce the cumulative pollution loadings and would provide continuing incentives for improvement even after primary and secondary standards had
been met, since taxes would still be paid on the remaining SO_2
emissions. Further, a nationwide sulfur tax would allow coal
conversion, so long as primary standards were met. The con-

verted plant would be paying the tax and would still have incentives to meet secondary standards or do even better.[18]

With a different set of technical characteristics, and far
greater complexity, the nation's program to control water pollution follows the same pattern. Prior to 1972, national strategy
was based on a four-stage process: federal approval of state-
established standards for water quality; state implementation
plans, requiring industrial firms and municipalities along a
river basin to reduce pollution discharges so as to meet the
standards; federal grants-in-aid for the construction of municipal waste-treatment plants; and court enforcement against
firms or municipalities whose failure to act caused a breach of
the standards.

For a host of reasons this approach failed. A principal cause
was that, on a river basin with many firms and municipalities,
it is impossible to pinpoint the source of a breach of water-
quality standards, especially given the rules of evidence in
judicial proceedings. The Federal Water Pollution Control
Act Amendments of 1972 adopted a drastically new approach.
The law required EPA to develop specific effluent limits on
water-borne pollutants for each type of industrial process, and
to issue permits to every industrial firm based on those limits.
By 1977 the effluent limits are to be consistent with the use of
"the best practicable control technology currently available";
by 1983 tighter limits based on "best available technology" are
to be imposed.[19]

In carrying out these objectives EPA is directed to take into
account "the age of equipment and facilities involved, the
process employed, the engineering aspects of the application
of various types of control techniques, process changes, . . .
non-water quality environmental impact (including energy

18. In 1971, President Nixon attempted to institute a tax on sulfur
dioxide emissions, but was unable to find a member of Congress to introduce it.
19. Public Law 92-500, sec. 301(b)(1)(A) and (2)(A).

requirements) and such other factors as the Administrator deems appropriate."[20] In addition, EPA must consider what is "economically achievable."[21]

There are 62,000 point sources of water pollution in the United States, of which 9,000 are major sources, with huge variation among them in the factors that EPA is supposed to consider—industrial processes, age of equipment, economic situation, and so forth.[22] EPA is therefore required to tailor its effluent regulations in some detail. Any given situation usually presents a broad range of possibilities for pollution reduction: changing the type of raw material used, altering the production process itself, modifying the characteristics of the product, treating the wastes before they emerge from the end of the pipe to reduce their polluting characteristics, or sending the pollutants through the sewer system and paying to have them treated at the municipal waste-treatment plant. Selecting the appropriate effluent limitation for each firm, in a way that will produce an efficient and effective overall strategy, depends on balancing these possibilities against their respective costs, taking into account the economic circumstances confronting each firm. To do this for 62,000 point sources of pollution demands omniscience from EPA.

By mid-1976, EPA had promulgated or was in the process of developing some 492 different effluent guidelines, and had issued 45,000 individual plant permits.[23] The language of the act leaves it wide open to legal challenges. In April 1976 EPA withdrew all its guidelines for organic chemicals (except for butadiene) because of a court challenge. Requests for administrative hearings are pending for more than one-tenth of all the industrial permits issued. Moreover, while the law envisioned state governments taking over the permit programs, after EPA

20. Ibid., sec. 304(b)(2)(B).
21. Ibid., sec. 301(b)(2)(A).
22. *Environmental Quality—1976: The Seventh Annual Report of the Council on Environmental Quality* (GPO, 1976), p. 15.
23. Ibid., pp. 12–13, 15.

approval and with EPA monitoring, only twenty-seven states have done so and, according to EPA, prospects that others will follow are very dim. Finally, an analysis of the program by the General Accounting Office found that most permits issued were not based on the final guidelines and that, in any event, firms were not adhering to the conditions of the permits.[24]

In effect, the current law sets up a central agency to determine a detailed control strategy for every polluting source, balancing environmental gains against economic costs. Difficult as this task is in a static context, it is dwarfed by the continuing problem of pacing the guidelines to economic growth and technological change. And the very nature of the controls discourages pollution-reducing technological change. The 1983 criteria base effluent limits on "best available technology." But will firms in polluting industries sponsor research or undertake experimentation to develop a new means of reducing pollution still further if its very availability will generate new and more stringent regulations?

The entire approach provides strong and positive incentives for polluters to use the legal system to delay progress toward effective cleanup. It forces a central control agency to make thousands of decisions resting on detailed knowledge it cannot possibly have and, even less, keep up with over time. And most important, it provides absolutely no incentives to firms and municipalities to channel technological innovation toward the efficient reduction of pollution.

It is possible, on the other hand, to put a common price— via an effluent charge—on each of the major forms of water pollutants. If the polluting side effects of industrial activity were priced, several consequences would follow. Depending on the size of the effluent charge, firms would have incentives to reduce pollution in order to increase their own profits, or to avoid losses. The higher the charge, the greater the reduction; hence the fee could be adjusted to achieve any desired set of

24. Ibid., p. 16.

water-quality standards. Firms with low costs of reducing pollution would reduce their waste discharges by more than firms with high costs of reduction, which is precisely what is needed to achieve any given environmental standard at the lowest national cost. Even when the standards were met, firms would still have incentives to look for ways of reducing pollution still further because they would be paying a fee on residual pollutants. And again, most important, there would be strong incentives throughout industry for the continuing development of new technology for reducing pollution.

Enough studies have been carried out on river basins to provide guidance on the magnitude of effluent charges needed to achieve particular water-quality standards.[25] But effluent charges are by no means the sole answer. Since we have had no experience with them they would have to be introduced gradually—you cannot create a large new market overnight. Regulations are already in force and they cannot simply be junked; effluent charges would have to supplement the regulations at first, not replace them. Moreover, as I stressed earlier, some exotic and highly dangerous chemical discharges will always have to be controlled by regulation rather than incentive. After all the qualifications, however, an incentive-oriented approach has a very large potential role, and its absence is very costly.[26]

25. Studies of the Potomac River Basin, the Delaware Estuary area, the San Francisco Bay, the Raritan Bay, the Miami River Basin in Ohio, and the Wisconsin River Basin, among others, have analyzed alternative approaches to achieving a specified set of water-quality standards. For a review of results of such research, see Allen V. Kneese and Blair T. Bower, *Managing Water Quality: Economics, Technology, Institutions* (Johns Hopkins Press for Resources for the Future, 1968).

26. In addition, there are some *perverse* incentives in the present law that must be suppressed. Because of depletion allowances and, in some cases, artificial rate advantages in transportation, virgin raw materials are favored over scrap and recycled materials. Present tax laws, allowing a special investment credit for specific waste-treatment equipment, give an artificial advantage to end-of-pipe treatment of wastes over other methods. Federal grants for the construction of municipal waste-treatment plants, and the lack of any assistance for operation and maintenance, encourage overbuilding and undermaintenance. The failure of many communities to charge appropriately scaled fees to industrial firms for treating their

Excessive regulation and failure to use other methods of correcting market failure characterize our approach to problems of occupational health and safety. The 1970 act establishing the Occupational Safety and Health Administration (OSHA) appears to assume that the essence of the problem lies in easily identifiable and preventable hazards, that relatively cursory inspections can detect the hazards, and that they result principally from the greed of unprincipled employers.[27] Both the structure and the budget of OSHA reflect this view: some 75 percent of the $118 million budget goes for compliance and enforcement; only 5 percent goes for safety and identification, analysis, and remedy of health hazards. But the number of industrial establishments is so large that even with such a budget OSHA has fewer inspections than some of the insurance companies that sell workmen's compensation. The average fine levied by OSHA for violations is about $25; only 523 out of 365,000 citations for violations were in the "willful, repeated, or imminent danger" category, and these carried an average fine of $1,100. According to the history of inspections to date, even a large plant is likely to be visited by an OSHA inspector only once every ten years.

OSHA has concentrated on industrial accidents and on obvious health-related problems. It regulates the trivial in exquisite detail, as these examples from the *Code of Federal Regulations* as of July 1, 1975, suggest:

Section 1910.35(b): Exit access is that portion of a means of egress which leads to the entrance to an exit.
Section 1910.25(d)(2)(vii): [out of 21 pages of fine print devoted to *ladders*] when ascending or descending, the user should face the ladder; [and] *(d)(2)(xx):* The bracing on the back legs of step ladders is designed solely for increasing stability and not for climbing.

---

wastes artificially encourages them to use that method of pollution control rather than to adopt changes in production processes or raw materials, which are often more efficient.
27. Cornell, Noll, and Weingast, "Safety Regulation," p. 502.

Section 1910.141(c)(1)(i): Where toilet rooms will be occupied by
no more than one person at a time, can be locked from the in-
side, and contain at least one water closet, separate toilet rooms
for each sex need not be provided. Where such single-occupancy
rooms have more than one toilet facility, only one such facility
in each toilet room shall be counted for the purpose of table J-1
[which specifies the minimum number of water closets according to the number of employees].

Section 1910.244(a)(2)(viii): Jacks which are out of order shall be
tagged accordingly, and shall not be used until repairs are made.

It is precisely the easily identifiable and correctable hazards
with which the market and the workmen's compensation system can deal reasonably well. Here there is no need for an
OSHA. Even a tenfold increase in its corps of inspectors could
not really enforce the regulations. In any event, OSHA cannot
touch the most important causes of industrial accidents. Sta-
tistical studies, for example, show that the turnover rate among
employees is the most important single factor in determining
injury rates.[28] To the extent that society wishes to spur reductions of such hazards, improvements in the workmen's compensation system or even the imposition of an "injury-rate tax"
would serve to raise the price upon such side effects and thus
harness private incentives to the task.

The true need for social intervention is in research, identification, dissemination of information, and regulation of the
much more subtle and uncertain health hazards, particularly
those involving long-term exposure to chemicals and irritants.
OSHA's charter and budget, however, neglect these aspects of
the problem in favor of a futile attempt to define and enforce
precisely those kinds of concrete safety measures that the
market can handle much more effectively.

Relying on regulations rather than economic incentives to
deal with highly complex areas of behavior, as we do for con-

28. Walter Y. Oi, "On the Economics of Industrial Safety," *Law
and Contemporary Problems,* vol. 38 (Summer–Autumn 1974), pp. 685–
87; Robert S. Smith, "The Feasibility of an 'Injury Tax' Approach to
Occupational Safety," ibid., table 2, p. 740.

trol of air and water pollution and industrial health and safety, has a built-in dynamic that inevitably broadens the scope of the regulations. Under an incentive-oriented approach—effluent charges, injury-rate taxes, or improved workmen's compensation—the administering agency does not itself have to keep abreast of every new development. The incentives provide a general penalty against unwanted actions. But if specific regulations are the only bar to prevent social damages, the regulating agency must provide a regulation for every possible occasion and circumstance. First it will take twenty-one pages to deal with ladders and then even more as time goes on. Social intervention becomes a race between the ingenuity of the regulatee and the loophole closing of the regulator, with a continuing expansion in the volume of regulations as the outcome.

Capital Grants

While we sometimes deal with complex problems of market failure by attempting to regulate side effects in detail, at other times we try to smother them in brick and mortar. Direct federal public works or federal construction grants to state and local governments are a favorite device for handling some kinds of market failure.

The principal means by which national policy has attempted to deal with traffic congestion in major urban areas has been through the provision of federal grants for the construction of subways and the purchase of buses and other mass-transit investments. At present, federal capital grants for mass transit amount to about $1 billion per year. But, as we saw, excessive congestion arises because individual auto commuters do not have to pay the full social costs of their driving: the delays each added commuter causes all other commuters are not priced. Capital grants for mass transit are unlikely to overcome this market failure for two reasons. In the first place, what limits the amount of commuter driving is not so much the monetary cost of the trip—gasoline, oil, repair costs, and so

forth—as the strain, tension, and other costs of congested driving. If the monetary cost of auto commuting were held constant while congestion were somehow reduced, that reduction
would be only temporary since more people would then decide
to drive to work. Building a subway, and subsidizing fares
through federal grants while holding the monetary costs of
driving ~~~^1 _____ ~~~ people who live near a
subwa _Decis. to subsid._ ~~~~~~ But the
result _be based on outputs should_ :ople
living _rather than inputs_ drive
their ~~~~)f the
initial reduction in traffic w~~~ ~~ Most
studies of the impact of mass transit indicate that ~. n fares
approaching zero probably would not make a major dent in
traffic congestion.[30] Only a sharp increase in the cost of driving,
sufficient to make monetary costs the limiting factor, is likely
to reduce congestion permanently.

Capital grants are a particularly poor means of subsidizing
mass transit. As seen by local transit authorities, such grants
lower the cost of capital inputs while not affecting the costs of
operations and maintenance. As a consequence, very large
capital-intensive systems, whose investment costs are high
compared with their operating costs, are given an artificial advantage over less capital-intensive bus systems. And even
with bus systems, the availability of large grants for the purchase of new buses induces transit managers to replace buses

29. At current monetary costs of both driving and mass transit there
would be an excess demand for driving, given lower levels of congestion.
Reduction in mass-transit fares would, everything else being equal, lower
that excess demand, but would be unlikely to wipe it out. More people
would thus drive, pushing congestion back up to the point at which it
eliminated the excess demand. If the initial congestion is already high,
and the demand for auto travel very elastic with respect to congestion and,
at that level of congestion, inelastic with respect to moderate changes in
monetary costs—all of which appear likely—then lowering mass-transit
fares will not reduce congestion very much.

30. See, for example, Leon N. Moses and Harold F. Wilkinson,
"Value of Time, Choice of Mode, and the Subsidy Issue in Urban Transportation," Journal of Political Economy, vol. 71 (June 1963), p. 262.

prematurely rather than to expend maintenance and repair funds (unsubsidized) to keep them running. One study of Chicago and Cleveland bus operations concluded that the federal policy of earmarking grants for capital investment stimulated wasteful decisions to replace buses much too soon, to the extent of absorbing 23 percent of the subsidy in unnecessary costs.[31] Whenever a decision is made to subsidize some activity, the subsidy should be based on outputs, rather than on specific inputs, to avoid biasing technical choices among inputs in a wasteful direction.

Congestion cannot be eased by ignoring the basic market failure that causes it—the fact that drivers do not bear the full social costs of their commuting. Heavy subsidies to alternative forms of transportation will not be sufficient. Auto commuting has to be positively discouraged. Stiff parking fees or commuting permit fees, while not perfectly efficient, could accomplish this task. Were these imposed, a subsidy to mass transit might be simultaneously undertaken to strengthen their effectiveness. The subsidy should be based on a specified amount per passenger trip or a percentage of fare-box revenues, or some combination of the two.[32] It should not be a capital grant.

The federal government now spends about $4 billion to $5 billion per year in grants-in-aid for the construction of municipal waste-treatment plants. The federal grants pay for 75 percent of the construction cost. Since municipal sewage is a major contributor to water pollution, what could be more

31. This problem is discussed further in William B. Tye, "The Capital Grant as a Subsidy Device: The Case Study of Urban Mass Transportation," in *The Economics of Federal Subsidy Programs*, A Compendium of Papers submitted to the Subcommittee on Priorities and Economy in Government of the Joint Economic Committee, 93:1 (GPO, 1973), pt. 6, pp. 796–826.

32. A flat subsidy per passenger trip would favor low-cost short-haul trips relative to high-cost long-haul trips, and be particularly favorable to inner-city residents. A subsidy calculated as a percentage of fare-box revenues would do the opposite; it would be particularly beneficial to suburban commuters using rapid rail transit, and most conducive to promoting competition with automobiles. Since both objectives are being sought, a subsidy scheme that combined the two approaches might be desirable.

obviously desirable than federal help in building treatment plants? But the "market" failure is not a shortage of investment financing for municipal construction. Rather, it lies in the fact that benefits from treating municipal wastes accrue heavily to downstream residents while the funds for building treatment plants are provided by taxpayers in the upstream community. Even if the federal government foots 75 percent of the construction costs, the remaining 25 percent and all of the operation and maintenance expenses must be paid out of local taxes. Since many of the benefits are enjoyed by voters in other communities, local governments have insufficient incentives to assume the necessary costs.

The result of the present arrangements is that many waste-treatment plants are overbuilt and undermaintained. Over half the plants studied by the GAO in 1970 provided substandard service, either because they were badly operated or because they were not designed to treat the waste load delivered to them.[33] Another study in the same year found that fully one-quarter of the waste-treatment capacity in metropolitan areas was less than half utilized.[34]

A federal effluent charge levied on pollutants discharged by municipalities would reflect the social costs that their actions imposed on other jurisdictions. It would give them the incentives to adopt the most economical mix of construction outlays and maintenance efforts to reduce effluents. The political obstacles in the way of levying a federal charge on "hard-pressed" local communities are obviously formidable. One way to defuse them would be to earmark the receipts for return to municipal treasuries in some way not tied to the amount of effluent they discharged.[35]

33. See Kneese and Schultze, *Pollution, Prices, and Public Policy*, p. 43.

34. Environmental Protection Agency, Water Quality Office, "Cost of Clean Water" (EPA, March 1971; processed), vol. 2, p. 72.

35. That is, an increase in pollutants discharged would raise the total sum paid by the community but not the sum it received back from the federal government. Some of the proceeds from the charge, together with

Federal Grant Programs

In the fiscal year 1976 the federal government provided some $60 billion in grants-in-aid to state and local governments. Of that amount $23 billion went for welfare, Medicaid, and other forms of payments to individuals; $14 billion for general revenue sharing or broad bloc grants with few federal strings attached; and $10 billion for three large capital-grant programs—highways, mass transit, and waste-treatment plants. The remaining $13 billion was devoted to a very large number of relatively narrow categorical grants, under which the federal government specifies in some detail how the funds are to be used.[36] One of the problems that characterize many of these categorical grants reflects a lack of correspondence between the nature of the grant and the "market" failure it was supposed to correct.

A special difficulty arises from a failure to distinguish between problems of supply and problems of demand in meeting a social objective. For example, starting about fifteen years ago the federal government began to take on responsibility for assuring that the poor and the disadvantaged had access to certain critical services—health care, manpower training, day care, and the like. In many cases existing institutions were unsuited to the delivery of such services in poor urban or rural neighborhoods, and in other cases no institutions existed at all. In virtually all cases the same grant was used both to provide the poor with financial resources to purchase such services and to create or improve the institutions that deliver them. In poor inner-city areas, where private physicians are scarce, neighborhood health centers are an attempt to provide a more attractive and effective alternative to the outpatient clinics of large city

---

those from industrial effluent charges, could be used to finance the large-scale public works that in some circumstances provide effective means of reducing water pollution (low-flow-augmentation dams, aeration of the waterway, holding lagoons, and the like).

36. Owen and Schultze, eds., *Setting National Priorities*, p. 360.

hospitals. Through grants the federal government furnishes the operating funds for such centers, and their services are made available without charge to inner-city residents. But in doing so the program runs into difficulties. In the first place, since the services are free (or require minimal fees), only the poor or near-poor are allowed to use them. This tends to create a two-class medical system. Second, the health centers are not subjected to the test of consumer acceptance; obviously, if they charge nothing they will be preferred to sources of medical care that do charge. The federal government thus not only supports the initial establishment of such centers, but is permanently committed to supplying the annual operating funds, and hence to exerting continuing oversight.

If, on the other hand, the two objectives were distinguished, a more reasonable approach could be taken. First, removing financial barriers to medical care for the poor can be accomplished by a system of medical insurance, either as a reform of the current Medicaid program or as part of a broader national health insurance system. Second, after providing the seed money to help new institutions like neighborhood health centers get started, the federal government could gradually withdraw the operating funds and require the institutions to charge fees covering costs. This would be no hardship for the poor, since their medical bills would be covered by federally supported insurance. But the neighborhood health centers would then have to stand the test of the marketplace, since potential clients would have the means to choose between them and other sources of medical care. Moreover, it would not be necessary to limit the centers' services to the poor, since everyone would be paying fees covering costs.

At least on an experimental basis, similar principles could be applied in other areas. If vouchers for manpower training programs were available to eligible recipients, government-sponsored and private training programs could compete for clientele. Government support could be limited to developmental help for innovative approaches or to isolated areas where private institutions are not viable. But all institutions would ultimately be required to stand the test of consumer acceptance. A similar approach could be applied to day care centers. And the same principle suggests concentrating federal support for higher education on direct assistance to students rather than on subsidies to colleges and universities.

Improving federal grant programs is not a simple matter; in particular, it cannot be accomplished merely by turning control over the grant funds back to state or local governments. In the case of the $23 billion in welfare, food stamps, Medicaid, and other grants for income support and health care, the central objective concerns income distribution. Basically this should be a national objective. Both equity and efficiency call for a more complete federalization of these programs. In the case of health centers, manpower training, day care, and the like, analysis does suggest that change is needed. The principal reform would be to place more choice directly in the hands of individuals.

Failure to Consider Incentive Problems

Across a wide range of areas, social intervention often fails, not because it relies unnecessarily on regulation or other command-and-control devices, but because in other ways it ignores the role of properly structured economic incentives for achieving social goals. One of these ways involves the perverse and antisocial incentives that some social programs themselves set up. Another is the failure to recognize how existing institutions channel private economic activity in the wrong direction.

The federal Medicare and Medicaid programs have historically reimbursed hospitals in a way that promotes, rather than discourages, the escalation of medical costs. Hospitals were reimbursed individually on the basis of the costs each incurred. As a consequence, there was no incentive to take measures to reduce costs, and given the sources of prestige in the medical profession, there was a positive incentive to add high-cost

technology and services. More recently, improvements in reimbursement policy have been undertaken to move the system
gradually away from an after-the-fact reimbursement of costs
toward one that does offer some incentives for cost control.
But progress is slow. And one concomitant of an under-
emphasis on economic incentives is an overemphasis on centralized controls that attempt to hold down costs by an ever-
growing body of detailed regulations.

Distorted pricing and incentives play a major role in creating urban problems. Virtually every city has a long-range
development plan. But every one of them is imposed on a
structure of investment incentives that invariably frustrates its
objectives.[37] We have already seen the consequences in congestion of failure to charge motorists the full social costs of
their commuting. Most cities set prices on sewer and water
services that do not properly reflect the cost of installing sewer
and water lines for new developments. Leap-frogging and
urban sprawl are in effect subsidized, since longer lines carry
no higher charges than close-in services. Profits from buying
and holding land for speculation are taxed as capital gains, at
rates that are far lower than those paid on ordinary income
from property improvements. Scarce entrepreneurial talent is
channeled into land speculation. The after-tax gains from buying land and then securing favorable variances in the zoning
code are much greater than those from the socially desirable
alternative of investing in property improvements under existing zoning. Given a limited access to capital, the investor in
inner-city residential property gets a high return by extensive
purchases of older property to hold, without improvements,
against escalation of land prices. Applying the same funds to
property improvements would yield income in the form of
rents, which are taxed at the higher rates applied to ordinary
income.[38]

37. A good survey of this set of problems is contained in Wilbur
Thompson, "The City as a Distorted Price System," in Harold M. Hoch-
man, ed., *The Urban Economy* (Norton, 1976).
38. And until recently the provisions of the tax code that favored

A FINAL NOTE

One cannot prove the existence of a behavioral law or tendency simply by reciting examples. And yet I think it is clear that we do limit the politically acceptable techniques for social intervention to a few predetermined approaches, and usually block out of our vision that class of alternatives that use market-like principles to achieve social objectives.

We try to specify in minute detail the particular actions that generate social efficiency and then command their performance. But in certain complex areas of human behavior, neither our imagination nor our commands are up to the task. We often see the causes of market failure at superficial levels—a physical shortage of mass-transit facilities, municipal water-treatment plants, or local health clinics—and instead of dealing with the root behavioral problem, try to build over it with construction grants. Instead of widening the area of individual choice for the poor and the disadvantaged by financial and institutional arrangements that give them alternative opportunities in day care, manpower training, health facilities, and the like, we tie the financing and the institutions together in a way that minimizes their range of choice. Consistently, where social problems arise because of distorted private incentives, we try to impose a solution without remedying the incentive structure. And equally consistently, the power of that structure defeats us.

If I am right that we tend to intervene in ways that are systematically biased in certain directions, then by definition the problem is not one of random error, or of personal incompetence on the part of the legislators and administrators. There must be some underlying reasons in the structure of our beliefs or our political systems why we act the way we do. It is to that question that the next chapter turns.

---

investment in property improvements were so structured as to discriminate against improvements to existing buildings.

IV

We rely on market incentives to bring us food, shelter, and clothing, but abjure them when it comes to producing clean air, occupational safety, and improvements in urban transportation. We segregate our approaches to social organization into two watertight compartments—command-and-control techniques for public intervention and economic incentives for the private economy. Yet there is a spectrum of alternatives between the two extremes waiting to be created through the public use of private interest. Why do we act as if the middle ground never existed? Why do we rely solely on one extreme for our techniques for social intervention?

The bias in the American political system—to intervene through direct determination of outputs by regulation and other forms of centralized bureaucracy—is deep-seated. There are, I think, several major causes of that bias, none of which can be changed by some simple modification of the political process.

If one accepts the views of James Buchanan and some of his colleagues in the public-choice school of political economy, only a radical constitutional revision that severely restricts the scope of allowable social intervention can deal with the problem.[1] His is a deterministic view: people vote only their pocketbooks, are exceedingly myopic about their own long-run interests, and inevitably end up voting for excessive government and output-oriented intervention. Normative economics, which tries to spell out some "desirable" course of action to correct market failures, is pie in the sky, and quite irrelevant in view of the way voters actually behave.

1. James M. Buchanan, *The Limits of Liberty: Between Anarchy and Leviathan* (University of Chicago Press, 1975).

In my judgment, this picture of the political process is far too narrow. People and legislators do vote their self-interest, particularly on matters that affect them starkly and directly. But they also have some views about the public good, quite apart from immediate effects upon themselves. People who vote against gun control and for a large defense budget, capital punishment, and balanced budgets at all times, are not simply trying to maximize their own economic gains. Votes against nuclear-power moratoria and strip-mining legislation cannot be predicted solely in terms of economic self-interest. Voters do form concepts of the public good that can be changed or modified, partly through widening the perception people have of their own self-interest and partly through political persuasion that itself creates new issues and alternatives. There is a crucial role for political leadership, not only to assemble narrow coalitions based on self-interest, but also to discover more effective solutions to market failures, articulate their advantages, and persuade voters. Politics can be, in some part at least, a creative process, not simply a deterministic response to the myopic self-interest of majorities or special-interest groups.[2] There is still room for normative economic judgments, based on an analysis of market failure. Trying to discern the underlying causes for the output-oriented bias of existing social intervention can be a worthwhile first step in an active political process.

THE INSEPARABILITY OF EFFICIENCY
AND EQUITY

In the first chapter I made the point that there is virtually no act of social intervention that does not impose losses on some

2. In an attempt to avoid what he believes are the inevitable excesses and inefficiencies of majoritarian processes, Buchanan is forced to propose very severe and, in my view, arbitrary constitutional limits on post-constitutional social action. He then has to rely heavily on a once-and-for-all property redistribution and an extensive creation of complex property rights to handle side effects.

people. Pollution control will reduce profits for some firms, in most cases temporarily, but in some instances permanently. Should outmoded transportation regulations be removed, the resulting reshuffling of the transportation system would bring losses to firms that were protected under the old system and to some communities whose value as shipping centers was sustained by artificially rigged transport rates.

An efficient social action will generate gains that exceed losses; if the losses exceeded the gains, the move, by definition, would not be efficient. In theory, therefore, the gainers from efficient social intervention could fully compensate the losers and still come out ahead. With no losers and some net gainers, the political obstacles to efficient social intervention would be minimized. The potentially divisive struggle over income distribution could be divorced from the problem of efficiency.[3] Designing efficient instruments of social intervention would present purely technical problems. Although these could still be formidable, and in the face of uncertainty require some nice judgments, one roadblock to efficient social intervention would be removed.

actually

In fact, of course, it is impossible in most situations to identify gainers and losers, to measure their gains and losses, and to devise means of transferring income from gainers to losers by means that themselves do not compromise efficiency. If a steel company responds to pollution controls by closing down some of its older coke ovens and building a new coke-oven complex, workers in the old installations will have to find new jobs. If, after only a short search, they find jobs at undiminished wages and at nearby locations, their losses are small. But suppose they find employment only at lower wages,

---

3. This is an oversimplification. Even if we could ensure that there would be no losers from a given social action, sharing the gains remains a problem. There are, for example, several alternative strategies for reducing sulfur emissions, each of which might compensate losers. But one strategy might spread the reductions fairly evenly over the nation, while another might concentrate the reductions in selected areas. Equity and distributional questions would still remain even if losers were compensated.

or only by incurring the expense of commuting 50 miles a day? How do we identify the short- and long-term losses when the outcome is likely to be different for each worker? What about the loss in tax revenue and retail trade in a one-factory community? And suppose the steel company shifts its purchase of coking coal from Kentucky mines to Pennsylvania mines?

Sometimes it is the problem of identifying the gainers and their gains that takes center stage. Decontrolling prices of domestic oil, and letting them move to equality with world oil prices, would promote efficiency. Imports are the residual source of oil supply. With domestic prices held below the world market as they are now, domestic consumption of petroleum is encouraged. Consumers currently make decisions based on the blended market price of oil, about $11 a barrel, but each added barrel of consumption costs the nation $14 to import, a $3 loss on every added barrel. Setting prices free to seek world market levels, however, would create a huge windfall for domestic producers with low-cost wells. If we knew the costs of production at each well, we could levy a tax well by well that still provided a generous return while capturing the windfall. But we cannot devise such a precisely calibrated tax. And without precise calibration, excessive taxes on high-cost wells would discourage domestic production and exploration. The upshot is that policies designed to promote an efficient energy program become hopelessly enmeshed in quarrels about income distribution.

Even if we had reached some broad political consensus on "fair shares" and overall income distribution, and had installed a system of progressive taxes and transfer payments to achieve it, efficiency measures would still be plagued by income-distribution problems. The overall measures might ensure, for example, that no one fell below the poverty line, and that generous unemployment compensation was available for those temporarily out of work. But what about the 50-year-old employee in a paper factory, earning $15,000 per year, who is forced to settle for an $8,000-a-year job as a result of an environmental decision that shut his factory down? Or the owner of a small trucking company whose lifetime savings are destroyed when the transportation regulations that protect his firm from widespread competition are removed? Establishing a reasonably egalitarian distribution of income by income classes does not eliminate severe losses or sharp gains to individuals as a consequence of social measures to improve efficiency.

(The problem of losses is exacerbated by the fact that the existing structure of laws and regulations is reflected in property values.) Farm subsidies raise the value of farmland; the farmer who buys his land *after* the subsidy is enacted pays for that subsidy in the cost of land and, taking that higher cost into account, ends up earning no more than he would with zero subsidy and lower land prices. The protection from competition that the regulations of the Interstate Commerce Commission afford shows up in the price that a new owner must pay for an existing trucking firm. And the value of residential land will reflect, in part, the value of the job opportunities in the local economy: if the one factory in a town is closed down, a home-owning worker who finds a job at equivalent wages in another town may still suffer a severe loss through the drop in residential values. Any special intervention, whether it scraps the old rules of the game or introduces new ones, necessarily destroys property values.

"Do No Direct Harm"

Incomes and property values are constantly being created and destroyed in the normal course of the changes that characterize a dynamic economy. But as chapter two stressed, social attitudes toward losses are much more rigid when it comes to losses directly imposed by government action. The rule of "do no direct harm" is a powerful force in shaping the nature of social intervention.

We put few obstacles in the way of a market-generated shift of industry to the South or the substitution of synthetic fibers for New England woolens, events that thrust large losses on individuals, firms, and communities. But we find it extraordinarily difficult to close a military base or a post office. We have elaborate procedures for changing zoning regulations and provide case-by-case adjudication where losses in property values may occur. But movements of private industry that destroy property values occur at will. When we intervene through regulation, we try to write the regulations and provide administrative discretion to take care of as much individual variation in circumstances as possible so as to prevent harms that can be immediately imputed to the regulation. Such regulations then grow at an exponential pace as experience in a far-flung economy steadily generates thousands of specific problems. More important, efficient ways of achieving results are often precluded by fear of some direct losses. The impersonal and blind-to-equity operation of effluent charges or of incentive-reimbursement schemes for hospitals under Medicare is eschewed in favor of regulations and case-by-case adjudication. When a large loss to a specific firm or industry threatens, we ease the regulations. The deadlines for emission-control targets on automobiles, carrying the brave threat of a $10,000 fine *per vehicle* for violations, have been postponed repeatedly. One recent study concluded that given the average fine levied for violations under the Occupational Safety and Health Act, it would pay a large firm to accumulate 400 violations before it was worthwhile to undertake the costs necessary to meet the regulations.[4]

In a similar vein, once government takes on responsibilities for providing services such as day care or skilled nursing-home care (under Medicare), an extension of the "do no direct

4. Nina W. Cornell, Roger G. Noll, and Barry Weingast, "Safety Regulation," in Henry Owen and Charles L. Schultze, eds., *Setting National Priorities: The Next Ten Years* (Brookings Institution, 1976), p. 500, note 53.

harm" principle inevitably leads to the assumption by government of responsibility for the quality of services delivered.
Increasingly detailed and ambitious standards of quality are
developed that shift the policing mechanism from consumer
choice to government regulations.

I do not want to suggest that social intervention, as currently practiced, avoids or compensates for all direct losses.
Any change brings losses to some. And however much we try
to avoid large direct losses, there are always indirect losses as
the effects of various policies work their way through the economy. But the extent of governmental moves to improve efficiency is sharply constrained, and the design of those moves
importantly limited, by attempts to obey the "do no direct
harm" rule. Because incentive-oriented approaches to social
intervention rely on decentralized reactions to prices, they
seem to deprive government of control of case-by-case results.
If nothing else, this would make legislators nervous. They
would have to forgo the opportunity to provide their programs with all sorts of adjudication procedures drawn up to
take care of specific losses. They would also forfeit the opportunity to second-guess administrators and to provide services
for constituents through intervention in administrative
decisions.

Rights and Duties versus Incentives

In the abstract there may seem to be no logic in our schizoid
view of losses—allowable for purposes of efficiency in private
markets, much less permissible for government actions. In fact,
our attitudes have an historical rationale. The constitutional
structures of most Western democracies arose, not as a response to political anarchy and a search for efficient collective
action, but in reaction to the excessive power of monarchs. In
the process, governmental power was not simply transferred
from monarch to parliament or congress, but hedged about
with safeguards. Protecting the rights of individuals in their

property, as well as in their persons, against the arbitrary exercise of power by government was a dominant concern both in framing constitutions and bills of rights, and in designing subsequent legislation that conferred particular powers upon government. That economic change might impose severe losses on specific individuals was a fact of life, as were hurricanes and floods. Until the Great Depression these losses were seldom the subject of politics. What was to be prevented was the imposition of losses by government.

Where government was called upon to act it was natural, in this environment, to think in terms of laws that specified the allowable actions in detail. And, as the complexity of the situations to be regulated grew, regulations were increasingly accompanied by various adjudicatory procedures, quasi-judicial bodies, administrative hearings, and other devices to adjust governmental actions to individual circumstances. Making law is still considered the province of lawyers. Some 60 to 65 percent of the members of the United States Congress have a legal background. Legal training necessarily, and quite rightly, concentrates on the specification of rights and duties in law and judicial precedent and on case-by-case adjudication in the light of the law and precedent. When society decides that social behavior ought to be changed, the lawyer goes about the task by setting forth the rights and duties of the parties involved, including the rights and duties of government. By the very nature of the process, the protection of individual equities is a prime consideration. A market approach, on the other hand, stresses incentives, not rights and duties. People or firms act in certain ways because their self-interest dictates doing so, given the existing set of incentives. Changes in social behavior can be accomplished by modifying the incentives that induce people to act. Individual equities are not a principal concern.

Where market failures can be handled by changes in the laws concerning property—for example, through improvements in the assignment of liability for side effects—the rights-

and-duties approach is an efficient one. But carrying over that approach to situations that demand much more complex forms of social intervention tends to produce output-oriented legislation—detailed regulation of outcomes accompanied by adjudicatory procedures to handle individual cases. In an age when government was not expected to intervene significantly in the marketplace the problem was not significant. But as both economic circumstances and public attitudes have changed to give social intervention a much wider sphere, the carryover of the legal approach takes on much greater importance.

Paradoxically, therefore, the historical development has carried our institutions full circle. The underlying principle that government shall do no direct harm and the legislative technique of carefully specifying rights and duties was, in part at least, an outgrowth of the movement to limit the power of government. But by applying the principle and the technique to situations in which social intervention must be pervasive and continuing, we have ended up extending the sphere of detailed governmental control far beyond what is necessary to accomplish the objectives we seek.

In the attempt to follow the "do no direct harm" principle, we have also begun to transfer more and more decisions about individual economic equities from the market to the government. Regulations, however detailed, cannot be written to cover all the individual situations that arise. The prevention of direct harms is pursued by incorporating some broad standards of "fairness" in the legislation and providing individuals with access to administrative hearing bodies and the courts for purposes of adjusting the regulations to their special circumstances. The legislation that assigns the Environmental Protection Agency the task of setting detailed effluent limits also requires its administrator to determine what is "economically achievable" and to take into account such things as "the age of equipment and facilities" (which necessarily varies from one firm to another). Specific outcomes, and the fortunes of particular firms and communities, begin to be determined on a case-by-case basis by the specific decisions of regulators, by administrative hearing panels, and by the courts—often by all three in sequence.

The application of general rules to individual circumstances through judicial interpretation is a vital part of governance. But too much of a good thing spoils the whole process. The toughest challenge to the political consensus necessary to hold a free society together arises when society itself has to make explicit decisions about the fate of particular groups and communities. Many of those decisions are now made by the market; government is not to blame for the outcome. Each economic change that produces efficiency does not have to be weighed on the scales against individual equities. As the volume of such decisions to be made by government grows, the strain upon the political fabric grows at least proportionately. Every decision is perceived as a loss, either by those who want the regulation enforced rigorously or by those who suffer its consequences. And that "loss" can be attributed directly to a specific government decision. As a result we may get the worst of both worlds: many efficient moves are avoided because of the fear of blame for losses, while the anger and frustration over the losses that inevitably do occur are focused on an identifiable governmental decision.

A second consequence of our current approach is that more and more economic decisions are made neither by the executive nor the legislative branch of government, but by individual judges. In determining, case by case, whether regulatory decisions are compatible with the standards set forth in the legislation, the courts must determine, for example, what is an "economically achievable" effluent limitation or what variation in limitations should be allowed for the "age of equipment and facilities." The exceedingly complicated weighing of benefits and costs, which the market and its feedback mechanisms carry out, is supplanted only in part by central regulatory bodies with their staffs of technical experts. It is also replaced by the decisions of countless judges, struggling under rapidly growing workloads. To deal with these cases, the courts have little technical assistance and must rely upon the technical content of adversary briefs. As a means of settling matters of personal and property rights, the adversary process has major advantages.[5] But it is a poor way to make highly complex economic policy.

There are, in summary, solid grounds for the historical emphasis on "do no direct harm" as a principle and the specification of rights and duties as a technique in spelling out the legitimate role of government. But their application to the newer forms of social intervention required by an increasingly interdependent society yields an output-oriented, command-and-control approach to social intervention that is not only inefficient, but productive of far more intrusive government than is necessary.

THE MYSTERY OF THE MARKET

By this time most congressmen and public administrators have had, sometime in their college career, at least one course in economics. Most of them, having presumably passed the course, are aware that the 10 million automobiles, 1½ million houses, 2 billion bushels of wheat, and 10 billion soft-drink bottles that were produced in 1976 represented quantities roughly coincident with consumer demands—not because some central authority ordered it, but in response to an intricate meshing of the signals and incentives provided by the price system. Prices, they learned, signaled consumer wishes to producers and the costs of fulfilling those wishes to consumers, and gave both the incentives to make appropriate choices.

In fact, I am increasingly convinced, no one but economists

5. Even here, however, it can be extended beyond its reasonable limits, as seems to be happening in the mushrooming field of liability cases— auto accidents, medical malpractice, and so on.

(and not all of them) really understands what is in this black box. Somehow the cars get into the showrooms and the loaves of bread onto the grocery shelves, but the whole thing is like an oft-repeated high-wire act: we don't really understand how it's possible, but it's been done so often we are no longer surprised.

A high price put upon some newly scarce resource causes it to be conserved, and at least roughly rationed to the highest-value uses. But the market produces these results by devious routes. Because the resource price is higher, goods that use a lot of it advance in price relative to goods that use little. Consumers therefore tend to shift their purchases away from goods that use much of the newly scarce resource. Producers who employ it now seek ways to economize on its use, and more effort will be devoted to finding new resource-conserving technologies. Alternative resources whose use was not profitable before the price increase will be employed as substitutes. The structure of production, consumption, and inventive activity will all begin to change in ways that conserve the scarce resource. But the particular changes that will occur in thousands of firms across the country cannot be catalogued in advance.

Because the way in which markets achieve results is both indirect and seldom understood, it is not surprising that more direct techniques of social intervention are usually chosen. If we want to achieve a specific reduction in polluting wastes, what could be more natural than specifying in law the desired outcomes and requiring people to meet them? If we want producers to adopt measures that reduce industrial accidents, why not simply require that the measures be undertaken? If there is too little commuting by mass transit and too much by automobile, what could be a more appropriate remedy than providing the money to build mass-transit facilities? If we think people should have more day care or training opportunities, why shouldn't the government establish and subsidize day care and training centers?

I find it hard to grasp the concept that electrons can best be described as a probability density function. To me, either they are there or they are not there. Luckily, I am not called upon to legislate on how to shift electrons about. In the same vein, it is devilishly hard to convince someone that an indirect, roundabout, and seemingly less certain way of accomplishing the objectives of social intervention should be preferred to a simple specification of required outcomes.

The Short Run versus the Long Run

One of the reasons why policymakers fail to appreciate how price changes can help achieve their goals is that prices in the free market act sluggishly to achieve *their* functions. Outside of agriculture and auction markets, prices do not change quickly to clear markets. In the short run, business firms and labor unions are themselves quantity adjusters. When sales fall and idle capacity appears, most industrial firms do not quickly cut prices. They hold them constant and reduce output to match the demand forthcoming at those prices. Wage differentials among firms and occupations are not rapidly altered to match the supply and demand for various types of labor. The economic system bases many of its day-to-day decisions on the maintenance of stable price and wage relationships. Recent theoretical developments in the "new-new microeconomics" are beginning to explain how this behavior is ultimately grounded in neoclassical maximizing principles.[6] But, plainly, in the short run the price system is not a delicate adjustment mechanism to keep demands and supplies neatly in balance. The fact that the observable day-to-day behavior of

6. John Hicks, *The Crisis in Keynesian Economics* (Basic Books, 1974); Arthur M. Okun, "Inflation: Its Mechanics and Welfare Costs," *Brookings Papers on Economic Activity*, 2:1975, pp. 351–90; William Poole, "Rational Expectations in the Macro Model," ibid., 2:1976, pp. 463–505; Robert J. Gordon, "Recent Developments in the Theory of Inflation and Unemployment," *Journal of Monetary Economics*, vol. 2 (April 1976), pp. 185–219.

the economic system does not match the textbook world of market adjustment cannot help but make it more difficult to defend the use of prices and pricing mechanisms as an instrument of social intervention.

In the long run, however, prices are a potent instrument. Given time, the economic system follows with incredible efficiency the price signals that society sends out. It is sometimes easier to demonstrate this from cases in which the price signals are wrong than from those in which they are right. In the naturally arid Imperial Valley, for example, water was brought in at great expense by irrigation works. But since the water is heavily subsidized and priced at absurdly low levels, one of the favorite crops in this land of scarce water is watermelons! By setting low prices on the possession of empty railroad boxcars, society has sent out a signal that efficient utilization of boxcars is unimportant, that boxcars are virtually a free resource. And behold! the average U.S. boxcar travels loaded only 7 percent of the time and covers the grand total of 50 miles a day. We develop a medical insurance system that, for various reasons, underwrites the cost of hospital stays (that is, puts a zero price on such stays for the individual patient) but does not do so for preventive medicine and physician office visits; and the entire structure of medical care gradually shifts toward hospital inpatient care. I have already noted that labor, always priced as a scarce resource, is steadily conserved in the production process, while environmental quality, on which we put no price, has always been wasted.

The problem is not that economic outcomes fail to respond to price signals. Over time they do, and with almost frightening efficiency. But in the short run, most market prices themselves change little, and only after substantial strains have built up. In turn, the behavior of business firms, workers, and consumers only gradually adjusts to new price patterns. As a consequence, observing the day-to-day behavior of private markets may provide a misleading and far from reassuring picture of the social efficacy of the pricing system.

Sharp Corners versus Smooth Curves

The world is not full of sharp corners and discontinuities. There is, for example, no one unique cost per unit of reducing the biochemical oxygen demand in industrial wastes; the costs of removing an additional unit gradually rise as a firm goes from 10 percent removal to 95 percent removal. Moreover, those costs vary from firm to firm. If an effluent tax were levied on each unit of BOD discharged, firms would compare the size of the tax with the costs of reducing discharges. They would remove BOD up to the point where the cost of reduction began to exceed the tax. The higher the tax, the greater the percentage of BOD removed. The specific response would be different for each firm, depending on its own costs. A common effluent tax levied on each firm within a river basin can thus be adjusted to achieve whatever degree of reduction is wanted. There is no threshold level of sulfur emissions below which we do not have to worry and above which damages are devastating; the degree of damage usually increases smoothly with the concentration of sulfur in the air. There is no necessity to make an all-or-nothing decision about whether a particular plant meets some precisely defined emission limit. Analogously, as a practical matter, there is no fixed amount of oil or coal or copper available in the ground; rather, as we gradually exhaust the better deposits, the costs of extracting additional resources steadily rise.[7] Industrial practices are subject to a wide range of modifications that, at gradually rising costs, produce gradually improving safety records.

In all of these kinds of situations there is no single set of technical solutions that yields the right answer for all firms and all situations. Efficiency demands that costs be balanced against gains in each case, taking into account the common characteristic that gradually rising costs buy gradually increasing gains—in pollution control, oil production, or industrial safety.

7. The improving technology of extraction sometimes offsets this rise.

Failure to recognize the continuity of most natural and economic processes contributes to the preference of legislators for output-oriented means of intervention. In the Senate floor debate over the Water Pollution Control Amendments of 1972, for example, effluent charges were briefly discussed. The floor manager of the committee bill argued against that approach on grounds that if the charge were set below *the* cost of cleaning up pollution, it would be ineffective since firms would obviously choose to pay the charge rather than undertake *the* cost of cleanup. Conversely, he argued, if the charge were set above *the* cost of cleanup, an unnecessary burden would be added to production costs and therefore to consumer prices.[8] Hence, it would be necessary to set the charge exactly equal to *the* cost of cleanup, an obviously impossible requirement.

One of the major efficiency gains from use of a price system is precisely its ability to induce individuals and firms to balance costs against gains under the particular circumstances confronting them in a world characterized by continuous adjustment possibilities.[9] The trick is to make sure that the costs and gains they confront also reflect, as far as possible, true *social* costs and gains. But if the concepts of continuous adjustment, rising cost curves, and declining demand curves are simply not understood, then the appealing simplicity of legislation that directly specifies outcomes will dominate the market alternative.

I may be stretching the point, but our unwillingness to deal in concepts of continuous adjustment when we design social intervention may stem not only from lack of technical understanding, but from the historical development sketched earlier. When the principal concern of legislators is the delineation of human rights and their protection against encroachment, the

8. *Congressional Record*, vol. 117, pt. 30 (1971), pp. 38828–31.
9. There is, consequently, little to be gained from using the price system where sharp discontinuities exist, and where we do not want a continuum of adjustments—for example, in the case of highly toxic chemical pollutants.

concept of continuous adjustment is not only irrelevant but dangerous. As Okun has pointed out, we explicitly forbid the buying and selling of votes, even though such an exchange could be a means for individuals to express gradations in the intensity of their political views. We do not allow trades for indentured service, or purchases of rights to free speech.[10] The sphere of human and political rights is full of sharp corners and discontinuities. While we still have to balance conflicting rights, we specify the balance in law; we do not permit individuals to reach some market-like equilibrium by trading along continuous adjustment curves. A concept that rests on a little bit more or a little bit less does not accord with the protection of human rights.

If my sense of history is right, for two hundred years social legislation has dealt with problems that did not require the delicate and continuous-adjustment mechanism that market processes can provide. Indeed, such tools were—rightly— deemed inappropriate and indeed destructive. In that context, it is easier to understand the current resistance to using these tools for the new kinds of social intervention.

The Creation of Markets

The markets that we actually observe did not spring forth full grown. In virtually every case the institutional forms and arrangements that characterize them are the Darwinian survivors of a number of alternative arrangements. Supermarkets did not appear suddenly as the successors of "Mom and Pop" grocery stores; they emerged gradually after a shaky start in the 1930s. Appliances are sold and repaired through a variety of arrangements that developed and competed with each other over the years. When new products are introduced, firms have to experiment with pricing structures and distribution outlets; but the volume of sales is small at the beginning and the consequences of initial errors are not critical to society. In no case,

10. Arthur M. Okun, *Equality and Efficiency: The Big Tradeoff* (Brookings Institution, 1975), p. 9.

however, does a price suddenly have to be set on some vitally important product that had never been priced before.

The literature on the efficiency of markets and on the advantages of using market-like processes for social intervention almost never recognizes the problem of creating markets de novo. It is easy to talk about marginal changes that can improve the efficiency of existing markets. In cases where no market exists, analysts usually compare the efficiency of full-blown pricing schemes (effluent charges, congestion fees, and the like) with existing regulatory approaches. In effect, they are asking policymakers to take a sudden leap into the dark— of a kind no private market has ever experienced. But in an environment where the indirect workings of market processes are not well understood anyway, this is simply begging for rejection.

In summary, two sets of factors seem to be responsible for the output-oriented nature of most social intervention. First, our political traditions place a high premium on preventing the government itself from imposing direct harms on individuals. We have typically accomplished this objective by carefully specifying the rights and duties of both government and individuals, and providing liberal opportunities for individual adjudicatory procedures. The application of these principles to areas of complex social intervention almost always results in attempts to specify outcomes directly through a combination of detailed regulation and judicial interpretation of particular cases. The "blind-to-equity" operation of an incentive system is seen by legislators as antithetical to traditional principles. Second, the roundabout and indirect process by which the price system determines outcomes is not well understood, and on the surface seems much less certain of achieving results than does the direct specification of outputs. The uncertainty about market-like approaches is probably heightened by a lack of professional attention to the very real transition problems that would accompany the deliberate creation of markets that never existed before.

V

ASIDE FROM analytic studies that attempt to demonstrate the superiority of market-like approaches in particular situations, can anything be done to enhance the political feasibility of such approaches? There are no hidden keys that will unlock closed political doors. But there are, I think, some general approaches that might help.

One of the secrets of getting more efficient social intervention lies in reducing the probability that efficient measures will impose large losses on some individuals, communities, or firms. There are several ways to prevent or cushion these losses.

In the ideal world of fully employed resources, economic change would still impose losses, but these losses would carry far less threat than they would in a world of high unemployment and unused capacity. Even in a tight labor market, with employers avidly seeking labor, a worker displaced by some efficiency-creating change might have to accept a job at lower pay. The market for his skills and experience might have been sharply reduced or destroyed. A community built around some locational advantage—a river site for a paper mill, say—would have less to offer other industries and, should the mill close down, the community might have to be satisfied with a lower-wage industry as replacement. These are real losses, but they relate to the advantages of skill or location that mean *extra* earning capacity beyond some basic level. Under full-employment conditions, there is little probability of losing one's livelihood altogether for long periods of time. Voluntary quit rates are high in prosperous times, as workers search for better opportunities. The number of job openings for those displaced by economic change far exceeds the net number of new jobs created each year.[1]

When labor markets are loose, unemployment high, and aggregate demand growing sluggishly, fears about job security deepen far more than the sheer increase in the number of unemployed would suggest. Job security jumps to the top of the list of public concerns. There is, of course, no neat correspondence between the state of the economy and the design of measures for social intervention. Yet the whole tone of an ebullient and prosperous economy is vastly different from that of a sluggish one. Fear of losses does not vanish by any means. But the environment within which public policy is made does change significantly, at least to the extent that matters of income security do not dominate other objectives.

One does not get full employment by snapping one's fingers. The obstacles to high-employment policy are not the subject of these lectures. But in weighing the costs and benefits of a high-pressure economy, we ought to keep in mind its contribution toward easing the political burden of pursuing efficient micro policies.

We spend far too little effort in identifying the losers from social interventions, and in trying to find ways of explicitly compensating them. Unanimously, economists who have studied transportation have concluded that freeing the industry from the bulk of existing regulations would substantially promote efficiency. But the political prospects for reform are virtually nil, for a simple reason. The losses during the transition from a regulated to a competitive structure would be tremendous for individual firms and communities. One of the major inefficiencies of the existing railroad structure, for example, is that railroads are forced to keep operating highly uneconomic routes and spur lines. Pressure to do so, and to maintain the existing regulatory structure, comes from com-

---

1. In 1973, for example, when the overall unemployment rate was 4.9 percent, voluntary quits in the manufacturing sector amounted to about one-third of the work force.

munities who believe that their economic fate is tied to the
rail service, which must in effect be subsidized by higher rail
rates for everyone. Most of them probably would be well
served by trucks if the railroad were allowed to close down un-
profitable service. But this general assurance from economists
does little to allay the fears of city fathers and their congressional lobbyists. If the move to shrink railroad mileage is truly
efficient, the benefits flowing to citizens in general through
cheaper freight service would be larger than the losses suffered
by individual communities. Why could not communities losing rail service have guaranteed access to trucking services
using subsidies through a transition period if necessary? To
avoid the large capital losses to owners who bought in at prices
already reflecting restricted competition, could we consider
buying back charters for trucking lines as the price of removing
restrictions on entry?

Usually proposals are made to devote the proceeds of effluent and emission charges to environmentally oriented government programs. But could not these proceeds be used to
reduce the corporate profits tax of firms according to an index
of the pollution problems of the industry to which they be-
longed? On the margin for each firm, the incentives of the
charge would not be weakened, but—at least roughly—the
losers would be partly compensated.

There is a limit to how far we can go in identifying and
compensating losers. We have to be careful that the compensation devices themselves do not become a subsidy to inefficiency. But we could, I am convinced, do far more to neutralize
the very strong, and very understandable, political pressures
against efficient methods of social intervention if we gave as
much analytic attention to the compensation problem as we
now do to efficiency. Economic and political analysis need to
be joined to develop a combined efficiency and compensation
strategy.

To increase the political acceptability of market-like approaches require not only more thought to reducing losses, but

also more effort on transition problems. Ten thousand technical studies demonstrating the superiority of emission and effluent charges as means of controlling many forms of pollution are not going to persuade legislators to junk existing regulations and switch in toto to a pricing approach. Only a charlatan would guarantee, for example, anything but the roughest guide to the appropriate fee structure. As I pointed out earlier, the markets and the pricing structures that we actually observe developed gradually and are continually being adjusted. No one was ever asked to design a full-fledged nationwide market from scratch. Indeed, one of the advantages of a price system is that, over time, it tends automatically to correct its own errors, and so at any one moment we observe prices that incorporate thousands of small prior adjustments.

Market-like instruments can supplant current command-and-control techniques only gradually. But not much thought has been devoted to dynamic strategies that, step by step, mesh a dwindling reliance on regulations with a cautiously expanding use of market instruments. Let not economists cast too much blame upon politicians for refusing to accept our marvelous instruments of efficiency: The fault lies not in our politicians but in ourselves.

When social intervention into new areas is considered, we start with a more or less clean blackboard. We don't have to erase an existing maze of command-and-control laws. But a different kind of problem then confronts us—impatience. Major political initiatives come only after the public has been persuaded that an important problem exists. Public interest groups concerned with the problem begin to convince more and more people that something must be done. The issue is taken up on the hustings by candidates and parties. A sense of urgency develops. After a sharp struggle, enough opposition is overcome to put together an effective majority. How can politicians then put before the public a ten-year plan for gradually developing a new market structure? "The mountains are in labour and come forth with a ridiculous mouse." Instead, the inevitable strategy is to enact ambitious legislation stipulating sharp and immediate results, and then to erode the regulations piecemeal with postponements and loopholes as problems develop. The very rhetoric and political process that moves us finally to get something done often puts us in a position where that something is done poorly. This line of thought points to a more general set of political difficulties that hinder efficient and effective social action.

The American political system has been a marvelously effective tool for providing both freedom and governance. Its institutions have been well suited for generating the compromises and accommodations about national issues needed in a large and heterogeneous society. But those institutions were especially designed to settle issues of value conflicts: Should we introduce a system of compulsory social security and what kind of system will be most acceptable to different groups with different interests and values? Should the federal government undertake a system of interstate highways and what should its relationship be with the states, which traditionally had responsibility for highway building? Should the spreading trusts and monopolies of the late nineteenth century be curbed by the federal government? The political process, with all its faults, achieved a nice balance between responding to the wishes of broad majorities and protecting the political freedoms of individuals. The fate of racial minorities was a glaring exception, to which we awoke scandalously late; but we did awaken and the system proved capable of acting.

It is no small thing to develop a political system that can reach consensus on matters involving basic values. But the political battle lines that are drawn are natural and easy ones, precisely because they involve values. Each side has its broad philosophical content—human rights versus social order; big government versus small government; federal responsibilities versus states' rights; full employment versus price stability; isolationism versus internationalism. There are good guys and bad guys. In the minds of the chief protagonists and their followers, the ethical content of the debate is large. The issues are understandable and free of technical complications. And, under these conditions, solutions that rest on specifying rights and outputs attract political support much more readily than those that call for complex changes in market processes.

As society has intervened in ever more complicated areas, however, and particularly as it aims to influence the decisions of millions of individuals and business firms, the critical choices have a much lower ideological and ethical content. For economic or social reasons, we may still want to move some area of decisionmaking completely out of the market and into the sphere of specified rights and duties. And the necessity will remain to form political battle lines around the very real question of whether to intervene at all. We cannot abandon the standard techniques and institutions for forming consensus and negotiating compromises among groups with widely different values. But how does an ingrained political process, which stresses value adjustments, come to grips with the critical choices among technically complicated alternatives when some of the very political techniques that move society toward a decision themselves make it difficult to pursue workable methods of intervention? Identifying heroes and villains, imputing values to technical choices, stressing the urgency of every problem, promising speedy results, and offering easily understandable solutions that specify outputs and rights— these are the common techniques of the political process whereby consensus is formed and action taken.

There is no obvious resolution to this dilemma. The suggestion that the political debate be confined to ends, while technicians and experts design the means once the ends have been decided, is facile and naive. Ends and means cannot and should not be separated. In the real world they are inextricably joined: we formulate our ends only as we debate the means of satisfying them.[2] No electorate or politician can afford to turn

2. Charles E. Lindblom, "The Science of 'Muddling Through,'" *Public Administration Review*, vol. 19 (Spring 1959), pp. 79–88; Charles L. Schultze, *The Politics and Economics of Public Spending* (Brookings Institution, 1968).

over the crucial question of how social intervention is to be designed to supposedly apolitical experts.

Therefore, I must end rather lamely. There is no instrumental solution to the dilemma. The only available course is a steady maturing of both the electorate and political leaders. How to intervene, when we choose to do so, is ultimately a political issue. I am convinced that the economic and social forces that flow from growth and affluence will continue to throw up problems and attitudes that call for intervention of a very complex order. How we handle those questions not only · will determine our success in meeting particular problems, but cumulatively will strongly influence the political and social fabric of our society. Even if it were politically possible— which it is not—we cannot handle the dilemma by abjuring any further extension of interventionist policies. But, equally, we cannot afford to go on imposing command-and-control solutions over an ever-widening sphere of social and economic activity. I believe—I have no choice but to believe—that the American people can deal intelligently with issues when they are painted in hues more subtle than black and white. Indeed, the political winds of the last few years can be read as a sign that the electorate is somewhat ahead of many of its political leaders. The voters are not disillusioned with government per se. But they are fed up with simple answers to complicated problems. They are ready, I think, for a more realistic political dialogue. Almost two centuries ago the arguments for the ratification of the Constitution were laid out in *The Federalist* papers—perhaps the most sophisticated effort at political pamphleteering in history. I have good reason to hope—and to believe—that today's voters can accept the same high level of political argument as the farmers, mechanics, and politicians of the eighteenth-century colonies.

Index

91

TYPESETTING
Monotype Composition Company, Inc., Baltimore

PRINTING & BINDING
Columbia Planograph Company, Washington, D.C.